*Charles Dickens's*

# David Copperfield

MODERN CRITICAL INTERPRETATIONS

*Charles Dickens's*

# David Copperfield

Edited and with an Introduction by

**Harold Bloom**

Viva Books

New Delhi | Mumbai | Chennai | Kolkata | Bengaluru | Hyderabad | Kochi | Guwahati

**First Indian Edition 2007**
**Reprinted 2011**

**VIVA BOOKS PRIVATE LIMITED**

- 4737/23 Ansari Road, Daryaganj, New Delhi 110 002
  E-mail: vivadelhi@vivagroupindia.net, Tel. 42242200
- 76, Service Industries, Shirvane, Sector 1, Nerul, Navi Mumbai 400 706
  E-mail: vivamumbai@vivagroupindia.net, Tel. 27721273, 27721274
- Jamals Fazal Chambers, 26 Greams Road, Chennai 600 006
  E-mail: vivachennai@vivagroupindia.net, Tel. 28290304, 28294241
- B-103, Jindal Towers, 21/1A/3 Darga Road, Kolkata 700 017
  E-mail: vivakolkata@vivagroupindia.net, Tel. 22836381, 22816713
- 7, Sovereign Park Apartments, 56-58, K. R. Road, Basavanagudi, Bengaluru 560 004
  E-mail: vivabangalore@vivagroupindia.net, Tel. 26607409, 26607410
- 101-102 Mughal Marc Aptt., 3-4-637 to 641, Narayanguda, Hyderabad 500 029
  E-mail: vivahyderabad@vivagroupindia.net, Tel. 27564481, 27564482
- First Floor, Beevi Towers, SRM Road, Kaloor, Kochi 682 018, Kerala
  E-mail: vivakochi@vivagroupindia.net, Tel: 0484-2403055, 2403056
- 232, GNB Road, Beside UCO Bank, Silpukhuri, Guwahati 781 003
  E-mail: vivaguwahati@vivagroupindia.net, Tel: 0361-2666386

*Published by arrangement with:*

Facts on File, Inc.
132 West 31st Street
New York NY 10001
USA



ISBN : 978-81-309-1873-0

Published by Vinod Vasishtha for Viva Books Private Limited, 4737/23, Ansari Road, Daryaganj New Delhi - 110 002. Printed and bound by Anand Sons, Delhi - 110 092.

# Contents

Editor's Note / vii

Introduction / 1
HAROLD BLOOM

The Moral Art of Dickens: *David Copperfield* / 9
BARBARA HARDY

David Copperfield: A Third Interesting Penitent / 21
CARL BANDELIN

David Sees "Himself" in the Mirror / 31
BARRY WESTBURG

Remembrances of Death Past and Future: A Reading of *David Copperfield* / 47
ROBERT E. LOUGY

*David Copperfield:* The Trial of Realism / 67
JOHN P. MCGOWAN

Mr. Peggotty and Little Em'ly: Misassessed Altruism? / 83
PHILIP M. WEINSTEIN

Secret Subjects, Open Secrets / 89
D. A. MILLER

Containing the Destructive Work of Remembrance / 111
NED LUKACHER

Chronology / 119

Contributors / 123

Bibliography / 125

Acknowledgments / 129

Index / 131

# Editor's Note

This book brings together a representative selection of the most useful criticism available on Charles Dickens's autobiographical novel, *David Copperfield*. The critical essays are reprinted here in the chronological order of their original publication. I am grateful to Guy Moppel and Susan Laity for their labors as researchers.

My introduction centers first upon what Ruskin called Dickens's mastery of "stage fire," and then finds in *David Copperfield* the origin of all subsequent portraits of the artist as a young man. The chronological sequence of criticism begins with the distinguished Barbara Hardy, whose concern is with the moral unity of *Copperfield*. Carl Bandelin, writing on the "Two Interesting Penitents" chapter, finds in David himself "the novel's most interesting, and most successful, penitent."

In an analysis of mirror imagery in *Copperfield*, Barry Westburg locates an aesthetic element in Dickens's vision of the education of the self, while Robert E. Lougy reads the novel as a series of reflections upon mortality. In an allied investigation, John P. McGowan relates memory to the flow of images in the narrative. In a discussion of the relationship between Mr. Peggotty and Little Em'ly, Philip M. Weinstein questions the critical assessment of the altruism of Peggotty's motives. D. A. Miller's highly original analysis examines the weird parallels between "the story of David's liberation" and "the story of his submission."

In this volume's final essay, Ned Lukacher reads the novel as Dickens's repetition of the primal scene, enacted as Murdstone's unprovoked beating of David, and David's desperate biting of his torturer's hand. Lukacher's deeply Freudian analysis serves to remind us again of Freud's assertion that the poets and novelists "were there before me."

# Introduction

Courage would be the critical virtue most required if anyone were to attempt an essay that might be called "The Limitations of Shakespeare." Tolstoy, in his most outrageous critical performance, more or less tried just that, with dismal results, and even Ben Jonson might not have done much better, had he sought to extend his ambivalent *obiter dicta* on his great friend and rival. Nearly as much courage, or foolhardiness, is involved in discoursing on the limitations of Dickens, but the young Henry James had a critical gusto that could carry him through every literary challenge. Reviewing *Our Mutual Friend* in 1865, James exuberantly proclaimed that "*Bleak House* was forced; *Little Dorrit* was labored; the present work is dug out as with a spade and pickaxe." At about this time, reviewing *Drum-Taps*, James memorably dismissed Whitman as an essentially prosaic mind seeking to lift itself, by muscular exertion, into poetry. To reject some of the major works of the strongest English novelist and the greatest American poet, at about the same moment, is to set standards for critical audacity that no one since has been able to match, even as no novelist since has equalled Dickens, nor any poet, Walt Whitman.

James was at his rare worst in summing up Dickens's supposedly principal inadequacy:

> Such scenes as this are useful in fixing the limits of Mr. Dickens's insight. Insight is, perhaps, too strong a word; for we are convinced that it is one of the chief conditions of his genius not to see beneath the surface of things. If we might hazard a definition of his literary character, we should, accordingly, call him the greatest of superficial novelists. We are aware that this definition confines him to an inferior rank in the department of letters which he adorns; but we accept this consequence of our proposition. It were, in our opinion, an offence against humanity to

> place Mr. Dickens among the greatest novelists. For, to repeat what we have already intimated, he has created nothing but figure. He has added nothing to our understanding of human character. He is master of but two alternatives: he reconciles us to what is commonplace, and he reconciles us to what is odd. The value of the former service is questionable; and the manner in which Mr. Dickens performs it sometimes conveys a certain impression of charlatanism. The value of the latter service is incontestable, and here Mr. Dickens is an honest, an admirable artist.

This can be taken literally, and then transvalued: to see truly the surface of things, to reconcile us at once to the commonplace and the odd—these are not minor gifts. In 1860, John Ruskin, the great seer of the surface of things, the charismatic illuminator of the commonplace and the odd together, had reached a rather different conclusion from that of the young Henry James five years before James's brash rejection:

> The essential value and truth of Dickens's writings have been unwisely lost sight of by many thoughtful persons merely because he presents his truth with some colour of caricature. Unwisely, because Dickens's caricature, though often gross, is never mistaken. Allowing for his manner of telling them, the things he tells us are always true. I wish that he could think it right to limit his brilliant exaggeration to works written only for public amusement; and when he takes up a subject of high national importance, such as that which he handled in *Hard Times,* that he would use severer and more accurate analysis. The usefulness of that work (to my mind, in several respects, the greatest he has written) is with many persons seriously diminished because Mr. Bounderby is a dramatic monster, instead of a characteristic example of a worldly master; and Stephen Blackpool a dramatic perfection, instead of a characteristic example of an honest workman. But let us not lose the use of Dickens's wit and insight, because he chooses to speak in a circle of stage fire. He is entirely right in his main drift and purpose in every book he has written; and all of them, but especially *Hard Times,* should be studied with close and earnest care by persons interested in social questions. They will find much that is partial, and, because partial, apparently unjust; but if they examine all the evidence on the other side, which Dickens seems

> to overlook, it will appear, after all their trouble, that his view was the finally right one, grossly and sharply told.

To say of Dickens that he chose "to speak in a circle of stage fire" is exactly right, since Dickens is the greatest actor among novelists, the finest master of dramatic projection. A superb stage performer, he never stops performing in his novels, which is not the least of his many Shakespearean characteristics. Martin Price usefully defines some of these as "his effortless invention, his brilliant play of language, the scope and density of his imagined world." I like also Price's general comparison of Dickens to the strongest satirist in the language, Swift, a comparison that Price shrewdly turns into a confrontation:

> But the confrontation helps us to define differences as well: Dickens is more explicit, more overtly compassionate, insisting always upon the perversions of feeling as well as of thought. His outrage is of the same consistency as his generous celebration, the satirical wit of the same copious extravagance as the comic elaborations. Dickens' world is alive with things that snatch, lurch, teeter, thrust, leer; it is the animate world of Netherlandish genre painting or of Hogarth's prints, where all space is a field of force, where objects vie or intrigue with each other, where every human event spills over into the things that surround it. This may become the typically crowded scene of satire, where persons are reduced to things and things to matter in motion; or it may pulsate with fierce energy and noisy feeling. It is different from Swift; it is the distinctive Dickensian plenitude, which we find again in his verbal play, in his great array of vivid characters, in his massed scenes of feasts or public declamations. It creates rituals as compelling as the resuscitation of Rogue Riderhood, where strangers participate solemnly in the recovery of a spark of life, oblivious for the moment of the unlovely human form it will soon inhabit.

That animate, Hogarthian world, "where all space is a field of force," indeed is a plenitude, and it strikes me that Price's vivid description suggests Rabelais rather than Swift as a true analogue. Dickens, like Shakespeare in one of many aspects and like Rabelais, is as much carnival as stage fire, a kind of endless festival. The reader of Dickens stands in the midst of a festival, which is too varied, too multiform, to be taken in even by innumerable readings. Something always escapes our ken; Ben Jonson's sense of being "rammed with life" is exemplified more even by Dickens than by Rabelais, in that near-Shakespearean plenitude that is Dickens's peculiar glory.

Is it possible to define that plenitude narrowly enough so as to conceptualize it for critical use, though by "conceptualize" one meant only a critical metaphor? Shakespearean representation is no touchstone for Dickens or for anyone else, since above all modes of representation it turns upon an inward changing brought about by characters listening to themselves speak. Dickens cannot do that. His villains are gorgeous, but there are no Iagos or Edmunds among them. The severer, more relevant test, which Dickens must fail, though hardly to his detriment, is Falstaff, who generates not only his own meaning, but meaning in so many others besides, both on and off the page. Probably the severest test is Shylock, most Dickensian of Shakespeare's characters, since we cannot say of Dickens's Shylock, Fagin, that there is much Shakespearean about him at all. Fagin is a wonderful grotesque, but the winds of will are not stirred in him, while they burn on hellishly forever in Shylock.

Carlyle's injunction, to work in the will, seems to have little enough place in the cosmos of the Dickens characters. I do not say this to indicate a limitation, or even a limit, nor do I believe that the will to live or the will to power is ever relaxed in or by Dickens. But nothing is got for nothing, except perhaps in or by Shakespeare, and Dickens purchases his kind of plenitude at the expense of one aspect of the will. T. S. Eliot remarked that "Dickens's characters are real because there is no one like them." I would modify that to "they are real because they are not like one another, though sometimes they are a touch more like some of us than like each other." Perhaps the will, in whatever aspect, can differ only in degree rather than in kind among us. The aesthetic secret of Dickens appears to be that his villains, heroes, heroines, victims, eccentrics, ornamental beings, do differ from one another *in the kinds of will that they possess.* Since that is hardly possible for us, as humans, it does bring about an absence in reality in and for Dickens. That is a high price to pay, but it is a good deal less than everything, and Dickens got more than he paid for. We also receive a great deal more than we ever are asked to surrender when we read Dickens. That may indeed be his most Shakespearean quality, and may provide the critical trope I quest for in him. James and Proust hurt you more than Dickens does, and the hurt is the meaning, or much of it. What hurts in Dickens never has much to do with meaning, because there cannot be a poetics of pain where the will has ceased to be common or sadly uniform. Dickens really does offer a poetics of pleasure, which is surely worth our secondary uneasiness at his refusal to offer us any accurately mimetic representations of the human will. He writes always the book of the drives. which is why supposedly Freudian readings of him always fail so tediously The conceptual metaphor he suggests in his representations of characte and personality is neither Shakespearean mirror nor Romantic lamp, neithe Rabelaisian carnival nor Fieldingesque open country. "Stage fire" seems to me perfect, for "stage" removes something of the reality of the will, yet only as modifier. The substantive remains "fire." Dickens is the poet of the fire of the drives, the true celebrant of Freud's myth of frontier concepts of that domain lying on the border between psyche and body, falling int matter, yet partaking of the reality of both.

## II

If the strong writer be defined as one who confronts his own contin gency, his own dependent relation on a precursor, then we can discove only a few writers after Homer and the Yahwist who are strong withou that sense of contingency. These are the Great Originals, and they are no many; Shakespeare and Freud are among them and so is Dickens. Dickens like Shakespeare and Freud, had no true precursors, or perhaps it might b more accurate to say he swallowed up Tobias Smollett rather as Shakespear devoured Christopher Marlowe. Originality, or an authentic freedom fro contingency, is Dickens's salient characteristic as an author. Since Dickens' influence has been so immense, even upon writers so unlikely as Dostc yevski and Kafka, we find it a little difficult now to see at first ho overwhelmingly original he is.

Dickens now constitutes a facticity or contingency that no subsequen novelist can transcend or evade without the risk of self-maiming. Conside the difference between two masters of modern fiction, Henry James and James Joyce. Is not Dickens the difference? *Ulysses* comes to terms with Dickens, and earns the exuberance it manifests. Poldy is larger, I think, than any single figure in Dickens, but he has recognizably Dickensian qualities. Lambert Strether in *The Ambassadors* has none, and is the poorer fo it. Part of the excitement of *The Princess Casamassima* for us must be that for once, James achieves a Dickensian sense of the outward life, a sens that is lacking even in *The Portrait of a Lady*, and that we miss acutely (a least I do) amidst even the most inward splendors of *The Wings of the Do* and *The Golden Bowl*.

*The Personal History of David Copperfield*, indeed the most personal and autobiographical of all Dickens's novels, has been so influential upon all subsequent portraits of the artist as a young man that we have to make a conscious effort to recover our appreciation of the book's fierce originality. It is the first therapeutic novel, in part written to heal the author's self, or at least to solace permanent anxieties incurred in childhood and youth. Freud's esteem for *David Copperfield* seems inevitable, even if it has led to a number of unfortunate readings within that unlikely compound oddly called "Freudian literary criticism."

Dickens's biographer Edgar Johnson has traced the evolution of *David Copperfield* from an abandoned fragment of autobiography, with its powerful but perhaps self-deceived declaration: "I do not write resentfully or angrily: for I know how all these things have worked together to make me what I am." Instead of representing his own parents as being David Copperfield's, Dickens displaced them into the Micawbers, a change that purchased astonishing pathos and charm at the expense of avoiding a personal pain that might have produced greater meaningfulness. But *David Copperfield* was, as Dickens said, his "favourite child," fulfilling his deep need to become his own father. Of no other book would he have said: "I seem to be sending some part of myself into the Shadowy World."

Kierkegaard advised us that "he who is willing to do the work gives birth to his own father," while Nietzsche even more ironically observed that "if one hasn't had a good father, then it is necessary to invent one." *David Copperfield* is more in the spirit of Kierkegaard's adage, as Dickens more or less makes himself David's father. David, an illustrious novelist, allows himself to narrate his story in the first person. A juxtaposition of the start and conclusion of the narrative may be instructive:

> Whether I shall turn out to be the hero of my own life, or whether that station will be held by anybody else, these pages must show. To begin my life with the beginning of my life, I record that I was born (as I have been informed and believe) on a Friday, at twelve o'clock at night. It was remarked that the clock began to strike, and I began to cry, simultaneously.
>
> In consideration of the day and hour of my birth, it was declared by the nurse, and by some sage women in the neighbourhood who had taken a lively interest in me several months before there was any possibility of our becoming personally acquainted, first, that I was destined to be unlucky in life; and secondly, that I was privileged to see ghosts and spirits; both these gifts inevitably attaching, as they believed, to all unlucky infants of either gender, born towards the small hours on a Friday night.

> I need say nothing here, on the first head, because nothing can show better than my history whether that prediction was verified or falsified by the result. On the second branch of the question, I will only remark, that unless I ran through that part of my inheritance while I was still a baby, I have not come into it yet. But I do not at all complain of having been kept out of this property; and if anybody else should be in the present enjoyment of it, he is heartily welcome to keep it.

> And now, as I close my task, subduing my desire to linger yet, these faces fade away. But one face, shining on me like a Heavenly light by which I see all other objects, is above them and beyond them all. And that remains.
>
> I turn my head, and see it, in its beautiful serenity, beside me.
>
> My lamp burns low, and I have written far into the night; but the dear presence, without which I were nothing, bears me company.
>
> O Agnes, O my soul, so may thy face be by me when I close my life indeed; so may I, when realities are melting from me, like the shadows which I now dismiss, still find thee near me, pointing upward!

No adroit reader could prefer the last four paragraphs of *David Copperfield* to the first three. The high humor of the beginning is fortunately more typical of the book than the sugary conclusion. Yet the juxtaposition does convey the single rhetorical flaw in Dickens that matters, by which I do not mean the wild pathos that marks the death of Steerforth, or the even more celebrated career of the endlessly unfortunate little Em'ly. If Dickens's image of voice or mode of representation is "stage fire," then his metaphors always will demand the possibility of being staged. Micawber, Uriah Heep, Steerforth in his life (not at the end) are all of them triumphs of stage fire, as are Peggotty, Murdstone, Betsey Trotwood, and even Dora Spenlow. But Agnes is a disaster, and that dreadful "pointing upward!" is not to be borne. You cannot stage Agnes, which would not matter except that she does represent the idealizing and self-mystifying side of David and so she raises the question, Can you, as a reader, stage David? How much stage fire got into him? Or, to be hopelessly reductive, has he a will, as Uriah Heep and Steerforth in their very different ways are wills incarnate?

If there is an aesthetic puzzle in the novel, it is why David has and conveys so overwhelming a sense of disordered suffering and early sorrow in his Murdstone phase, as it were, and before. Certainly the intensity of the pathos involved is out of all proportion to the fictive experience that comes through to the reader. Dickens both invested himself in and withdrew from David, so that something is always missing in the self-representation. Yet the will—to live, to interpret, to repeat, to write—survives and burgeons perpetually. Dickens's preternatural energy gets into David, and is at some considerable variance with the diffidence of David's apparent refusal to explore his own inwardness. What does mark Dickens's representation of David with stage fire is neither the excess of the early sufferings nor the tiresome idealization of the love for Agnes. It is rather the vocation of novelist, the drive to tell a story, particularly one's own story, that apparels David with the fire of what Freud called the drives.

Dickens's greatness in *David Copperfield* has little to do with the much more extraordinary strength that was to manifest itself in *Bleak House*, which can compete with *Clarissa*, *Emma*, *Middlemarch*, *The Portrait of a Lady*, *Women in Love*, and *Ulysses* for the eminence of being the inescapable novel in the language. *David Copperfield* is of another order, but it is the origin of that order, the novelist's account of how she or he burned through experience in order to achieve the Second Birth, into the will to narrate, the storyteller's destiny.

# The Moral Art of Dickens: *David Copperfield*

*Barbara Hardy*

*David Copperfield* is a Victorian novel, and its powers and defects have to be seen in the context of its age. It is a bildungsroman or novel of education, based on models neither purely nineteenth-century nor purely English. Its powers and defects spring from the character and art of its creator, and in this novel, his "favourite child," he was keeping very close to life, and the relation between author and novel is a complex and interesting one. It is an autobiographical novel, though this term will only guide our understanding and appreciation if we use it to describe not only the obvious reporting of actual happenings and details in Dickens's life, but also its sensitive openness, not disconnected with the report of actuality, to the personal drives of dissatisfactions and desires. If it can be called autobiographical, it must also be called inventive, and its inventiveness creates a very individual emotional range, both comic and serious, which has very little to do with visible sources, contexts, and models, but which must be praised, criticized, and above all, *recognized,* as centrally and typically Dickensian. Like most works of art, it is less than perfect, and something has to be said about its unevenness.

A few words about its Victorianism. There is less explicit criticism of Victorian society in this novel than in Dickens's other writings: his eye was on his own domestic and spiritual adventures, and not on social injustice. Being the man he was, seeing his own life necessarily involved some social criticism, but this emerges implicitly, and often unconsciously. There are

---

From *The Moral Art of Dickens*. © 1970 by Barbara Hardy. Oxford University Press, 1970.

some exceptions. The book contains some hard nuggets of topical concern, usually extractable and conspicuous: the plea for prostitutes and their reclaim, the satire on the law, the criticism of model prisons, the interest in emigration. These mostly appear as tractlike forms within the continuum of the novel, not digressions but certainly statements in a different mode. We may feel that the treatment of Em'ly's seduction suffers from being part of a generalized case about fallen women, but we are most likely to applaud the formalized little coda about prison reform, which allows the three villains to take a final bow and create a new piece of satirical irony. But these embedded tracts are few. More typical and more interesting is the revelation of Dickens's implicit social attitudes, often remaining well below the conscious level of criticism. In Dickens's other study of psychological growth, *Great Expectations,* the psychological concerns are socially expressive: Pip's humiliations, ambitions, illusions, snobbishness, gentlemanliness, and fall and rise, are all recognizable social symbols. The novel is at once a portrait of an individual character and a strong generalization, and Dickens consciously and ironically and movingly manipulates the fusion. But in *David Copperfield,* because he is closer to his hero, and in a position where he found it hard to be distanced and objective, the relation of psychology to social expression is markedly different. David often reveals—or rather *betrays*—Victorian limitations which the author does not see but which the modern reader most certainly does. David's dissatisfaction with Dora's housekeeping, for instance, is very plainly both characteristic of his sex and age, an expectation and a need which it never occurs to him to question or criticize. He takes very great pains to show David's painful attempts, after intolerant and demanding mistakes, to accept Dora as she is, and the tolerance and compromise are clearly meant to be seen as meritorious. In a sense they are, but what we, as modern readers, are likely to do is to set aside the limited assumption that every man deserves a good housekeeper, and sympathize with the undated and moving residue—David's difficult decision to accept another human being for what she is, which is not what he wants or needs. Or again, David's chief professional characteristic as an artist, in one of the strangest portraits of an artist ever written, seems to be hard work. The modern reader, associating a rather different set of values with the artist's life (whether he likes them or not does not matter), is likely to find it difficult to sympathize with this emphasis. Not that we can quite call it a Victorian concept of the artist: Wilhelm Meister, before David Copperfield, and Will Ladislaw or Hans Meyrick, after him, are quite close to the Bohemian stereotype which makes us expect the artist to be irrational, unstable, rootless, unhappy, wounded. Dickens himself fits our idea of the wounded artist with his creative bow much better than David Copperfield, but here again, we are likely to extract the Victorian admiration for industry, placed in a curious collocation, and accept the less dateable part of the portrait, that humane curiosity and shrewd observation which Dickens picks out from the very beginnings of the novel, as characteristic of David as an embryonic novelist. Such socially determined elements, of which the author is unconscious, play an interesting part in the novel, but they form only a part of it, and are happily combined with concerns and interests which can still command our sympathy.

There are some moments when Dickens seems to make the imaginative effort to move outside a socially limited obtuseness. Up to a point, we may feel superior and critical before Dickens's unsympathetic portrait of Uriah Heep, whose servility and unctuousness are plainly created by an illiberal society. But here Dickens manages devastatingly to make his hero feel the dull distaste and yet recognize the social implication: Uriah is the creature of his time, and placing the social responsibility where it belongs makes him no more likeable. Dickens is perhaps not totally able to draw the moral, though he struggles. After the last revelation of Heep's "infamy," David speaks in terms both priggish and, I think, inaccurate:

> "It may be profitable to you to reflect, in future, that never were greed and cunning in the world yet, that did not do too much, and over-reach themselves. It is as certain as death."

To which Heep's reply, despite the moral implications of his own downfall, seems clearly the last word, in realism and social insight, after the simplifications and wish-fulfilment of David's innocence:

> "Or as certain as they used to teach at school (the same school where I picked up so much umbleness), from nine o'clock to eleven, that labour was a curse, and from eleven o'clock to one, that it was a blessing and a cheerfulness, and a dignity, and I don't know what all, eh?" said he with a sneer. "You preach about as consistent as they did. Won't umbleness go down?"

Since the novel ends with umbleness going down splendidly, albeit in prison, this riposte seems to mark a rare division between Dickens and David. It certainly marks Dickens's imaginative recognition of the social significance of Heep and the socially determined nature of the ethics of industry. Dickens is not perhaps entirely behind the comment, for he does use his art to celebrate the certainty of vice's downfall, and he does elsewhere preach the blessedness and dignity of labour pretty loudly, but the passage marks, I think, a fruitful uncertainty, a movement of the critical imagination beyond those historical limitations which operated on it. It is always dangerous to patronize Dickens's social complacency: he may not be consistently critical, but the very unpredictability with which he can jump over his own Victorian fence makes it safer to expect subtlety and insight rather than blindness.

Our response certainly does not always fulfill his expectations of sympathy and approval, though there were Victorian readers who also shrank from some of his excesses of pathos and solemnity. But there is no doubt that our tolerance of some areas of feeling, or some kinds of demands on feeling, have radically shifted. When David sees Agnes as the figure in the stained-glass window, "pointing upward," the Excelsior effects are unlikely to come off, not just because our attitudes to women have become happily less ideal, but because Dickens is counting on a context of religious reverence to bring his readers halfway to meet him, which is likely to send a fair number of his modern readers racing off in the opposite direction. I do not think we can here attack Dickens for exploiting religiosity and counting on a too easy generalized or stock response. He may have been cold-bloodedly manipulating the reader—a dated stock response can scarcely be tested for sincerity—but it is more likely that he was quite naturally and uncritically making and expecting stock responses in a way that we all do, in creating art or in daily life. Later novelists are not necessarily more particularized and concrete in their rendering of feeling, but are drawing on expectations of different stock responses. We were, for instance, especially ready to sympathize with the inhibited stoic who fears the insincerities of the language of strong feeling. Who can doubt that Hemingway sometimes relied on the stock response to the collocation of the laconic and the nobly sincere, just as Dickens relied on the stock response which gives a double measure of feeling for the collocations of religion and woman, or woman and child? Dickens expected his readers to admire hard work, domestic efficiency, a high degree of rationality, and competence, and did not usually take the trouble to argue, objectify, or particularize such merits. James Joyce expected his readers to sympathize with outsiders, exiles, and victims of persecution, and also perhaps relied to some extent on stock responses in his creation of Leopold Bloom.

I do not suggest that our judgment should be overruled by the tolerant efforts of our historical imagination. I think the religious/feminine ideal presented in Agnes is repulsive, and the childlike/feminine/sickly appeal of the dying Dora only slightly less so. We must admit the problem of the man, as well as the habits of the age. There were good biographical reasons why Dickens should tend to sentimentality when he was treating death, children, and ideal women. George Eliot is very much more tolerable on the domestic ideal (by which Mrs Poyser and Dinah pass, and Hetty fails) but tends to be lachrymose on the subjects of brother and sister and very small children. Dickens's own Mrs Bagnet in *Bleak House* is a very splendid instance of the domestic ideal, and Paul Dombey and the young David Copperfield are particularized where Little Nell is left blank, to be filled in by the stock response. *David Copperfield* is flawed by vagueness and inflated demands, but it has plenty of vivid, particular, and entirely successful demands to make on our feelings.

Take, for instance, the childhood scenes of the early parts of the novel. They are not only vivid, recapturing the closeness, sharpness, and disproportionate power and mystery of the child's sensations, but are perfectly adapted to the character-study Dickens is creating. David is a sensitive child, and his sensitivity is to make him terribly vulnerable to adult cruelty and adult neglect. It is also to make him alert and alive, with the curious observant eye of an insecurity sharpened not only by intelligence but by the inability to take any experience for granted. Dickens's psychology of childhood, so often rightly praised, must be seen as part of the psychology of the whole character, a study in isolation and the novelist's imagination. Once more, we need to admit that the novel is uneven. David can be seen as a complex thinking and feeling character, but only up to a point.

Dickens has been often praised, in recent years, for his "episodic intensification," that power of creating strong, moving, and convincing details, moments, and scenes. Critics like Gwendolyn Needham and Edgar Johnson have praised *David Copperfield* for its powers of thematic unification and control of idea. It has been praised for its coherent analysis of "the undisciplined heart," the phrase in which Annie Strong sums up her youthful, irrational, and amoral feeling, and which stirs David to self-recognition and diagnosis. Almost every character, problem, and episode can be seen as an illustration of this theme. I do not want in any way to deny the novel this unity of subject. It is there, and most explicitly so. What I do want to deny is that the idea, and its unifying function, is a source of strength. G. K. Chesterton, whose criticism combines effusiveness with much insight, said that Dickens's characters were often implausible, but still possessed the power to shake us profoundly. I believe that it is not so much the moral and psychological study of the heart and its training, which gives *David Copperfield* its strength and its vitality, as the intense and local shafts which strike deep as human insights, honest revelations, and dramatic communications.

As a novel of education, I would not put *David Copperfield* in the same class as *Middlemarch, The Portrait of a Lady*, or *Sons and Lovers*. These novels show the difficulty of being human, the complexity of human identity and relationship. From reading them, we do not return to a world whose flux and uncertainty is shatteringly different. In *David Copperfield* we are shown a very neat graph of progress: once David sees that his heart is undisciplined, the path ahead is fairly smooth and straight, and Dickens, here as elsewhere, illustrates what seems to me to be a moral and psychological fallacy, the fallacy of identifying diagnosis with remedy. Once Scrooge, Martin Chuzzlewit, David, and Pip arrive at self-knowledge, they can march on to improvement and conversion. Seen as a bildungsroman, the novel's fable shows us very little that carries over into the encounters with life. And the simplifications often rest on evasion within the novel. The actual concept of the disciplined heart seems rather crude, and owes much, I believe, to the impression made on us by another and easier kind of discipline, the discipline of action. We see David's grit and professional industry emerging from the ordeal set him by Betsy Trotwood, his fairy godmother; and by a kind of sideways shift, we may well ignore the absence of much dramatic evidence for the emotional discipline that Annie Strong speaks of. I say "dramatic evidence": both Annie and David tell of, but do not show, their change of heart. Annie's narrative is a summary of action and feeling, made in retrospect when she confesses to her husband. David's narrative is made to the reader. We are meant to feel and approve David's attempts to discipline his own demands for comfort, rational companionship, and a profound love, and to accept the deficiencies of Dora and of his marriage. Behind the pages of narrative obviously lie the novelist's own hard and fatigued attempts to live with his own marriage. But the toughness and wryness of this experience of accepting uncomfortable life remain unrealized, in terms of the art of fiction. It is dealt with in summary, not shown in action, and though a novelist like Henry James can give to such summary, in the harsh vision of Isabel Archer in *The Portrait of a Lady*, what he himself called "vivacity," inner action is not Dickens's strength. The report is not only severed from incident, but also undramatic as report. We *see* how he takes his "woodman's axe" and "cuts down the trees" until he comes to Dora—here the duplicity of the term "discipline" is plain, I think—but in the key passages in chapter 58, "Domestic," we are only *told* that David gave up the attempts to change his wife. He says that the old unhappy feeling haunted him but was undefined, haunted dreams but did not wreck the present:

> It remained for me to adapt myself to Dora, to share with her what I could, and be happy, to bear on my own shoulders what I must, and be still happy. This was the discipline to which I tried to bring my heart, when I began to think.

Dickens is really only approaching, and then retreating from the idea of showing the disenchanted life. Dora goes on holding his pen, they correspond with Agnes, speculations about another possible life remain outside, conveniently undisturbing. He is touching on a marvellous subject for the psychological novel, but only touching on it.

He chose to summarize, to evade, and then to cut the knot with Dora's death. Many a marital problem in Victorian fiction has to be solved by the Providential death. Dorothea Brooke benefits from this convention every bit as much as David Copperfield: it was left for Henry James, in *The Portrait of a Lady*, to refuse to cut the knot as Dickens and George Eliot had done, but before we praise him too highly at their expense, we should remember that he finished the novel before showing us Isabel Archer's undismissed marriage.

Both George Eliot and Charles Dickens knew in their own experience the pains of enduring an unloving marriage, she through Lewes's marriage, Dickens through his own. In recognizing the author's invocation of his own Providential plot-control to kill off Dora and lead the way to Agnes, we cannot simply refer to conventions in fiction. Convention and personal fantasy meet here: we are accustomed to speak of the maturity of great art, to see works of art as therapeutic, to applaud the use of technique as discovery, to equate good art with objectified feeling, and bad art with the gratifications of fantasy. Such standards leave us with a handful of novelists and even with these we will find spots of commonness, even with them it may often be the sparsity of biographical materials which makes us speak confidently about their powers of objective realization. All I should like to say here is that some artists, like Charlotte Brontë, and Dickens, work very close to life in some respects, and very far away from it in others. The so-called autobiographical novel is likely to contain chunks of actual report (the school in *Jane Eyre*, the reading, childhood isolation, and neglect in *David Copperfield*) and episodes of wish-fulfilling fantasy (the union with Rochester in *Jane Eyre* and the death of Dora and the marriage with Agnes). We might add the childhood parts of *The Mill on the Floss* and the final union with Tom. It is significant that these novels tend to employ two distinct modes, one a realistic, the other a fantastic, often vaguely religious and idealized symbolic mode. Here are three novels where, we are tempted to say, the psychological realism is confined to the childhood sections, the fantasy of symbol and convenient plotting for the adult section. This is only roughly true: there are moments in the adult sections of all three where truth and subtlety are operative. The pressure of fantasy need not always show itself in vagueness or authorial magic of the kind which produces deaths and conversions and happy marriages at the wave of a wand.

In *David Copperfield* fantasy is at work, shaping relationships, feelings, and climaxes that belong to dreams and wishes, and that tend to lie outside the clear scrutiny of the shaping artist and the self-critical man. It is particularly difficult to communicate and criticize what our longings create: the "Eureka-feeling," the sense of romantic affinity, and the relief at the end of struggle, all contribute to the religiosity and unparticularized feeling in this novel. Dickens invokes both religious and natural symbolism to express the desires and their wished fulfilments: it is in the Alps, amongst grandeur, isolation, and elevation, away from "the world," that he discovers the rock on which his love is founded. The very image of the rock is significantly both Wordsworthian and Biblical. We may well borrow other men's profundities and sublimities to convey what we most want and least know. As Arnold Bennett said, the writer's craft is open to many temptations. Dickens is not the only artist to use his art to reflect and distort and re-create an unsatisfied life.

The results are not only inflated and unconvincing symbols and actions. What are we to say of the comic transformation of the feckless and ponderous Mr Dickens, Senior, into Micawber, and the comic conflation of Dickens's wife and his sweetheart, Maria Beadnell, in the figure of Dora. Dickens uses comedy in the reforming of experience by fantasy. We should note that it is reformed: he was conscious enough of the biographical elements in the novel, and as with most artists, there were some of these elements which he most skilfully controlled and disguised. The real Mrs Dickens wrote a cookery book when she was sixteen and, as Margaret Lane observes in an essay in her book, *Purely for Pleasure* (London, 1966), "would have had no patience with Dora Copperfield." While we talk crudely of the gratification of killing off a wife in fiction, we must also recognize the disguises which imagination can put on, consciously or unconsciously.

We may say that Dickens was dealing with a theme, or adopting a pattern, to which his genius was not suited, or we may say that the closeness of the novel to his discontents and desires made the large moral pattern one very difficult for him to substantiate. However, as I said earlier, this does not mean that the novel has no psychological interest. The psychological interest tends to be rather erratic, appearing in spots rather than stretches, especially once we follow David into the adult world, but it is arrestingly present. I would pick out small details first. In the chapter I have mentioned, "Domestic," where there is so much summary and evasion, we find revealing and moving dialogue with Dora, which shows how good Dickens can be when he is reticent. David tells her in terms that are perhaps as tactful as the subject allows, that he has been trying to change her, has seen his error, and has decided not "to try any more." Dora's response is one of the many small details that make her character more subtle than most critical accounts of it admit:

> "It's better for me to be stupid than uncomfortable, isn't it?" said Dora.
>
> "Better to be naturally Dora than anything else in the world."
>
> "In the world! Ah Doady, it's a large place!"

One moment like this is more delicate and moving than all the loudly whispered hints about her last talk with Agnes. The reader who responds to the novel should be alert to this side of its treatment of people—the reticence, the suggestion, the feather-movement. Other fine moments are of course less quiet. Take, for instance, the night when Uriah Heep sleeps in David's room, a scene dramatically conveying the physical revulsion inseparable from the jealousy which helps to give the adult David the sexual dimension he mostly lacks. In a sense, this episode reminds one of Conrad's *The Secret Sharer,* and taken in combination with the parallels in David's position and Uriah's —poor boys struggling upwards—and with the sexual gloating of Uriah and the lofty purity of David's attitude to Agnes, seems to suggest a kind of Id/Super-Ego tension, I would not suggest that we take this very far, but the relationship between the two men seems to reveal more than is ever made explicit, and the study of David's loathing for Uriah is one of the most powerful insights in the novel. (I do not know if anyone has observed the Biblical origins of their names, but I would suppose that this was an instance where Dickens was not conscious of all the ironies of the associations: Agnes is as far from Bathsheba as Molly Bloom from Penelope, but David certainly wins her from Uriah.) Dickens's treatment of David's feeling for Uriah and Steerforth is much more moving, I suppose because more particularized, than his treatment of the feeling for Dora and Agnes, in the one case distanced by comedy, in the other inflated by a compound of ideals.

I make this brief mention of such moving psychological detail for two reasons: first, because I have criticized the subtlety and interest of the central psychological theme of the undisciplined heart, and must make it plain that I do not consider that Dickens is incapable of treating emotion and relationship; second, because I may be in danger of suggesting that the novel's comic mode is its only source of strength. In fact, the comedy is involved in the weaknesses, too, if only in a negative sense. Those characters in Dickens who are totally exempt from comedy tend to be the unrealized and insubstantial creatures: David himself, like Micawber, Traddles, and Betsy Trotwood, has a vitality that seems in part to derive from the exposure to comic, as well as to serious, analysis. But the comic parts of the novel make a strong contribution to local effect: the vitality of farce and language is both brilliantly funny in details of scene and character, and excellently imitative. Dickens's jokes do not explode and leave no trace. When Micawber speaks, the style is the man:

> "Under the impression," said Mr Micawber, "that your peregrinations in this metropolis have not as yet been extensive, and that you might have some difficulty in penetrating the arcana of the Modern Babylon in the direction of the City Road—in short," said Mr Micawber, in another burst of confidence, "that you might lose yourself—I shall be happy to call this evening, and instal you in the knowledge of the nearest way."

Micawber's celebrated "in short" does not merely show up the inflation and grandiose circumlocution of his great flights, it cuts them short, and modifies their grandiosity. The really hollow men in Dickens, like Chadband in *Bleak House,* irritate the reader into deflating and translating their flights; Micawber's very lack of hollowness is shown in his ability to deflate himself, and the stylistic deflation that follows the "in short" almost always signals the descent to practical matters. The reader who properly attends to the style will not feel too startled at Micawber's final triumphs. The comedy here, as in other characters, is subtly deceptive and subtly revealing. The reader has to learn, with David, to see beneath the comic simplifications, to learn, for instance, that Mrs Micawber's elasticity is not simply comic, but guarantees her much-vaunted but far from hollow constancy, or that Betsy Trotwood's comic spinsterishness has more in it than meets the eye. Dickens is learning to use comedy, not simply for farce and satire, but characteristically, and most originally, to create surface effects and then trip us into feeling the depths beneath. His apparently endstopped jokes, and his apparently static caricatures, are dynamic and complex.

This kind of comedy is appropriately used in a novel of memory, a novel which explores the past, reenacts it, and explores its meanings. The past sensations and feelings are presented as things remembered, and the effect of the double vision of David the past child, and David the man in the present, works in the same way as the comic duplicity. The rhythm of the novel depends largely on the relation between the time past and time present, a relation which is made very emphatic in the several "Retrospects" where, by a stroke of what I would call linguistic imagination, Dickens uses the present tense to express what is most visibly presented as the rapid passing of time in the past, a present tense which speaks with a sad and faintly mocking voice of what was vivid and now has faded, a perfect vehicle for all the ironies of nostalgic remembering, reliving, questioning, and burying. Some of the most complex writing, which blends comedy and pathos, is in these passages, and it is in them, I believe, that the strongest source of the novel's unity is revealed. *David Copperfield* is a chronicle of "the silent gliding on of . . . existence," the memory of "the unseen, unfelt progress of . . . life," of "the river," and "the journey"; and the gliding is halted, the progress held up, the river stopped, and the journey interrupted, in these four great punctuating chapters, arrestingly coming at the ends of instalments, where the theme is stated, the summary made, the symbol movingly created out of that "historic present" which uses the language of time present to dramatize time past. It is the unity of feeling, that concept of form used by Schlegel and Coleridge to answer the rigidities of their neoclassical predecessors, that seems most appropriately invoked to describe the structure, the subject, and the appeal of *David Copperfield*.

# David Copperfield: A Third Interesting Penitent

*Carl Bandelin*

The "Two Interesting Penitents" chapter of *David Copperfield* has traditionally been considered an example of what seems to be Dickens's occasional willingness to sacrifice literary coherence to his nonliterary interests. Sylvère Monod, for example, writes, "If Dickens, in 1850, had taken an active interest in fire brigade stations or lunatic asylums, David might have found Littimer and Heep in another kind of establishment. So, once more facts whose appearance in the novel is not justified by any inner necessity are less convincing and sound less truthful than some imaginary circumstances." Barbara Hardy, expressing a different though equally negative response, patronizingly excuses Dickens's "lapse," suggesting that of the "hard nuggets of topical concern" in the novel, "usually extractable and conspicuous . . . we are most likely to applaud the formalized little coda about prison reform." Whether or not Dickens is occasionally guilty of such lapses may indeed be a fair question, but in this case, I suggest, the judgment is mistaken. David Copperfield himself is a penitent in the last half of the novel, repenting his earlier mistakes, trying to mend his ways, and ultimately finding salvation in Agnes's love. The Penitents chapter plays an important part in the narration of this process. It is comic, to be sure, but its ironies are not merely a source of humor for the reader: they actually effect a significant change in David's consciousness, for it is immediately after this interlude that his obsessive self-denial begins to wane and his union with Agnes becomes possible. To understand this change,

---

From *Studies in English Literature 1500–1900* 16, no. 4 (Autumn 1976). 

then, and the part the Penitents play in it, is to understand more fully the whole of David Copperfield's *Bildung*, or development.

The central problem for the Dickens protagonist in general is to acquire the ability to live creatively and humanely in the world. This often requires the resolution of conflicts between healthy self-awareness and inordinate self-consciousness. To be blind to the effects of one's actions is the greater danger: as Dickens says of James Harthouse in *Hard Times*, "publicly and privately, it were much better for the age in which he lived, that he and the legion of whom he was one were designedly bad, than indifferent and purposeless. It is the drifting icebergs setting without any current anywhere, that wreck the ships." But to be preoccupied with one's self is also unsatisfactory. Thus Arthur Clennam in *Little Dorrit* is "free" to live only after he has lost his self-consciousness about aspects of his past which are irrevelant to his own life. Esther Summerson in *Bleak House* suffers a similar psychological paralysis until she too ceases to be self-conscious about the circumstances of her birth. Even Bella Wilfer in *Our Mutual Friend*, in whose case the point is made most explicitly, must experience her "Glaring Instance" rather than merely be told of her faults: she does not learn her lesson, but rather comes to know it.

The nature of this process is especially clear in *David Copperfield*. During his childhood, David is quite naturally egocentric and rarely considers that his actions might affect others. This attitude is relatively harmless in David's early youth; indeed, it is he who is usually mistreated—by his stepfather, by waiters, coachmen, and schoolmasters. But as David grows older the implications of his actions become more serious, and yet he remains blind to them until his world suddenly collapses. After the deaths of Dora, Steerforth, and Ham, and the emigration of the Peggottys and Micawbers, David retreats to Switzerland where for the first time he begins seriously to examine his place in the world.

The losses for which David grieves during this Dark Night of the Soul are in part the result of his failure to foresee the effects of his actions; his recovery, in turn, is partly the result of the greater consciousness he acquires while alone and undistracted. The process is not simple, but Dickens has carefully given us the clues necesary to understand David's psychological condition. The crucial point is that David suffers more than grief alone: he reaches a true psychological crisis as—finally—he feels his share of responsibility for the deaths of his wife and friends. But although David becomes aware of his weaknesses, he cannot understand their consequences, and his penitence is therefore only half-successful. The profundity of his feelings of guilt carries him beyond the necessary "healthy self-awareness" to an excessive introspection, as he tries to comprehend his feelings. The distinction between known grief and unknown feelings of actual guilt will, I think, help explain the nature of David's recovery and the function of the Penitents chapter in that recovery.

David initially identifies the shock he feels during his Dark Night as grief, and sees no ambiguity:

> If my grief were selfish, I did not know it to be so. I mourned for my child-wife, taken from her blooming world, so young [Dora]. I mourned for him who might have won the love and admiration of thousands, as he had won mine long ago [Steerforth]. I mourned for the broken heart that had found rest in the stormy sea [Ham]; and for the wandering remnants of the simple home, where I had heard the night-wind blowing when I was a child [the Peggottys].

At first glance, however, the magnitude of David's emotion seems excessive. He loved Dora, but at the same time his marriage was an acknowledged burden. He felt a certain fondness toward Ham, but certainly not equal to his love for his own mother, nor even much greater than the fondness he felt for Barkis, both of whose deaths he had endured more easily. He had introduced Steerforth into the Peggotty household, but no one held him responsible for its disintegration. Even Steerforth's death had not previously overwhelmed David, who, looking at the corpse on the beach, could think of him "at [his] best." Nor can even the sum of these—weighty as it is—fully account for David's breakdown. His initial shock is a "heavy sense of loss and sorrow"—that much is to be expected. But David's feeling of desolation grows, and seems for a time to threaten his life. Clearly he is experiencing something even more powerful than grief.

It is important therefore to notice the language in which David recalls his feelings:

> It was a long and gloomy night that gathered on me, haunted by the ghosts of many hopes, of many dear remembrances, many errors, many unavailing sorrows and regrets. . . . There are some dreams that can only be imperfectly and vaguely described; and when I oblige myself to look back on this time of my life, I seem to be recalling such a dream.

This language describes the world of the unconscious—or rather, of thoughts and memories hovering near the boundaries of consciousness. These imperfect and vague descriptions are not explanations of David's errors, for he never fully understands his mistakes. They are, however, symbolic indications of the sources of David's guilt feelings. As Taylor

Stoehr has remarked of the dream-qualities of *Great Expectations,* "the whole structure of the plot depends on the interplay of meanings at the level of dream. Pip's story from beginning to end is both a sequence of events that happen to him and a projection into reality of his own desires and fears." In *David Copperfield,* fantasy and event are causally related: David's fantasies affect his behavior, and his behavior affects events. His emotional response to particular events is disproportionate to his intellectual understanding of them, but rightly so, for he is responding not only to the event, but to the whole fantasy-behavior-event complex. David is responding, that is, to his own part in the tragedies he has witnessed. The most important of these are the seduction of Emily and its consequences (especially the deaths of Steerforth and Ham) and the death of Dora. A brief analysis of these events will help clarify the nature of David's emotions.

David's childhood infatuation with Emily is related explicitly; his continuing fascination is equally clear. But these later feelings are mixed. Returning to Yarmouth as a young man, David is pointedly aware of the social distance between himself and Emily, and is pleased that she is to marry a man in "her own station of life." Observing her through a window at Omer and Joram's, however, he sees "much of her old capricious coyness . . . but with nothing in her pretty looks . . . but what was meant for goodness and for happiness." Emily's coyness has the predictable effect of sustaining David's romantic fascination, but this presents a problem: Emily is too "good" to be trifled with, and yet she is socially ineligible as the object of honorable love. David's desires, then, are quite complex: he must win Emily's romantic attention but keep this from reaching fruition, and at the same time he must—because of his own honorable affection—avoid bringing any pain to Emily or her family. Fantasy and event, however, appear to remain separate, for any possible action by David is preempted by Steerforth's seduction of Emily.

The match between Steerforth and Emily is curiously appropriate. Emily had always wanted to be a "lady," and Steerforth was, in David's eyes, the quintessential gentleman. Moreover, as early as his days at Salem House David had associated Emily's budding sexuality with Steerforth's strength and charm. This sexual association would naturally be enhanced by the older Steerforth's urbanity (especially his adeptness with waiters, wine, and cigars) as well as by David's own lack of self-confidence. By inducing Steerforth to visit Yarmouth, then, David seeks to please both of his friends and thereby win more of their affection for himself. His fantasies, however, are more sinister: David is "arranging" for Steerforth to commit in deed the transgression which he himself commits only in wish. Steerforth is thus David's surrogate in his quest for Emily's attention.

I do not mean to suggest that David's real intentions are conscious—clearly they are not. But it is equally clear that David is given ample warning of Steerforth's plans. Steerforth himself, on several occasions, strongly hints to David that he is about to do something of which he is less than proud, and Agnes has pointedly warned David about his "Bad Angel." Most explicit is Miss Mowcher's game of Forfeits: Steerforth has just remarked that Emily "was born to be a lady," and Miss Mowcher replies, "What's that game at Forfeits? I love my love with an E, because she's enticing; I hate her with an E, because she's engaged. I took her to the sign of the exquisite, and treated her with an elopement; her name's Emily, and she lives in the east? Ha! ha! ha! Mr. Copperfield, ain't I volatile?" Mr. Copperfield, strangely, does not reply—he seems not to have heard. David is callow, of course, but his incomprehension here is not the result of his inexperience. Dickens has taken considerable pains to reveal that David refuses to see what is plainly before him, and thus refuses to prevent the imminent seduction.

The seduction itself, acceptable to David as an unconscious fantasy, is intolerable in fact: "I felt the shock again. I sank down in a chair, and tried to utter some reply; but my tongue was fettered, and my sight was weak." This shock is David's reaction to a deeper sense of guilt than that which one would expect him to feel for simply introducing Steerforth to Emily. It is a guilt serious enough to give David the impulse to "go down upon [his] knees, and ask their pardon for the desolation [he] had caused."

Just as David had "wished" the seduction of Emily, he now "wishes" the death of Steerforth, as a purge of his own responsibility for the seduction:

> I never had loved Steerforth better than when the ties that bound me to him were broken. In the keen distress of the discovery of his unworthiness, I thought more of all that was brilliant in him, I softened more towards all that was good in him. . . . Deeply as I felt my own unconscious part in his pollution of an honest home, I believed that if I had been brought face to face with him, I could not have uttered one reproach. . . . I felt, as he had felt, that all was at an end between us. What his remembrances of me were, I have never known—they were light enough, perhaps, and easily dismissed—but mine of him were as the remembrances of a cherished friend, who was dead.

There seems, at first glance, to be a confusion of time here. These are David's thoughts as they were immediately subsequent to the seduction, and in the narrative Steerforth is still alive. Dickens has not lost control, however; the tenses are quite as they ought to be. David has already forgiven his friend by imagining him dead and choosing to remember him only in his unfallen state.

This solution is momentarily shaken by the shock David experiences when he witnesses the physical death of Steerforth and sees his fantasy become event. Some of David's shock seems to be carried through into his Dark Night, but his reflections by and large retain this feeling of reconciliation, and reveal once again the disjunction between acceptable fantasy and intolerable fact. David / Dickens (the retrospective David) had manipulated the narrative, interrupting it with retrospective chapters, to create a series of discrete "former states" in which characters can be isolated and identified. He is thus able to make the two Steerforths concrete, and to work out his reconciliation in a formalized way. He "kills" the fallen Steerforth, and lets the innocent Steerforth live. But although David can consciously make this distinction, unconsciously he cannot, and this too contributes to the discrepancy between David's thoughts and emotions during his Dark Night. He remembers the states in which he and his friends were innocent, but he feels his whole past, including his guilt.

The potential power of David's unconscious feelings can be more clearly seen in the case of Ham's death, for here they nearly become fully conscious. The storm at Yarmouth, the community whose faith David had violated, has a curious effect on him: "Something within me, faintly answering to the storm without, tossed up the depths of my memory and made a tumult in them. Yet, in all the hurry of my thoughts, wild running with the thundering sea,—the storm and my uneasiness regarding Ham were always in the foreground." Dazed and confused by the storm and his memories, David is powerless, as though in a dream. His conscious mind clings to the activity around him. In Ham's determined face, looking out to sea as it had the night of Emily's seduction, David sees only danger, but he feels the implications of his earlier actions, and is overwhelmed. He can only stand by helplessly and watch them worked out.

This delicate division between conscious thoughts and unconscious feelings is most apparent in David's marriage to Dora, and her death. Here the process of fantasy becoming event is dramatically concentrated. Critics have generally regarded the marriage as a source of several important lessons for David, but note that once these lessons are learned the marriage is fated. Dora, that is, must then leave the narrative so that David can move on. But Dora's death, I suggest, is not merely a matter of technical convenience; it is inevitable on the basis of circumstances within the novel itself. Dickens does not clumsily write Dora out of David's life; rather, David, and Dora herself, do it for him.

David begins to "kill" Dora soon after the wedding, by trying to change her. Dora, of course, is nothing if not a child, and to make her old and wise is to make her no longer Dora. But David tries to do just this, first by teaching her to be more practical, and then when Dora proves too childish to be taught, by pompously trying to "form her mind" into something more serious. "When Dora was very childish . . . I tried to be grave. . . . I talked to her on the subjects which occupied my thoughts; and I read Shakespeare to her. . . . I accustomed myself to giving her, as it were quite casually, little scraps of useful information, or sound opinion." When this too fails, David has what seems to be a revelation, that Dora will always be a child and that he must accept and love her as such. This insight is followed by another revelation, however, for David now sees that he can never be fully satisfied with a child-wife, and that he needs just the opposite: he needs Agnes, whose age is limitless and whose wisdom is, to David at least, infinite. He now begins to resent Dora more seriously, and to wonder what would have happened had he and Dora never known each other, but he stoically resolves to keep his growing dissatisfaction a secret: "It remained for me to adapt myself to Dora; to share with her what I could, and be happy; to bear on my own shoulders what I must, and be still happy." David, that is, is writing Dora out of his life: "poor, giddy, stupid Dora"—as she calls herself—must never know his serious thoughts.

But poor, giddy, stupid Dora has powers of perception that David never suspects. Earlier, she had seen right through his attempts to change her, and she waited patiently for him to see the futility of his projects. Now she sees the futility of the marriage itself—more clearly even than David—and she too sees that David truly needs Agnes in order to be fulfilled. As she lets her will to live dissipate, and herself with it, she sends for Agnes and "bequeaths" David to her. Dora then dies, of her own free will, but also at David's unconscious behest.

David, of course, had not consciously wished Dora to die. Rather, he wished that she did not exist as his wife, and he says of these fantasies, they "slumbered, and half awoke, and slept again, in the innermost recesses of my mind." But although David's wish is unconscious, his overt self-discipline and self-sacrifice contribute to Dora's loss of vitality, and therefore to her death. Fantasy once again becomes event. David's reaction to Dora's death, then, encompasses even more than grief: it also encompasses the shock with which he unconsciously responds to the consequences of his wishes and actions.

Dora's death is followed closely by the deaths of Steerforth and Ham, and the emigration of the Peggottys and Micawbers. These several losses come so quickly that David is temporarily prevented from feeling the full impact of any one of them, for he is immediately occupied with the next. After the emigration, however, there is nothing to distract him—no activity to buoy his spirits—and his crisis now begins as he is overwhelmed by the sum of his emotions. "From the accumulated sadness into which I fell, I had at length no hope of ever issuing again," David notes; he is oppressed by sadness, but also by his anxiety about even deeper, incomprehensible emotions: "For many months I travelled with this ever-darkening cloud upon my mind. Some blind reasons that I had for not returning home—reasons then struggling within me, vainly, for more distinct expression—kept me on my pilgrimage." David feels the weight of his sins, but he cannot understand these feelings: grief took him to Switzerland, but his unknown guilt keeps him there.

The central agent in David's recovery is, of course, Agnes. She transmits, through her letters, the hope and faith in himself that David requires if he is to reenter the world. "She gave me no advice," writes David, "she urged no duty on me; she only told me, in her fervent manner, what her trust in me was." But although Agnes's influence enables David to break the major part of his paralysis, his hopelessness, it intensifies another sort of paralysis: David's overtly self-conscious repentance. He now recalls the tag lines of the lessons he has learned about his "undisciplined heart," his lack of "firmness," and his impulsiveness, and he recognizes that he himself is partly to blame for his present misery. David's repentance is sincere, but misdirected, for by concentrating on the simple morals of his lessons he ignores their true meaning and attacks the symptoms rather than the cause of his earlier misdeeds. His lament for his former lack of self-control is still inward-directed, still egocentric, and for the moment prevents the expression of the outward-directed love which will eventually save him. David at this point rejects love, vowing never to reveal his love for Agnes, and thus obstructs his own salvation. This is the paralysis that is broken in the Penitents chapter, for not until his visit to Creakle's prison does David discover the incompleteness of his repentance.

When David emerges from his Dark Night he seems to have recovered: he is physically and mentally healthy, he has been sincerely repentant, and he has learned his lessons well. He is as fully conscious of this as is the reader. Moreover, he is proud of his new strength of character: "I endeavoured to convert what might have been between myself and Agnes, into a means of making me more self-denying, more resolved, more conscious of myself, and my defects and errors." At his aunt's house, before seeing Agnes again, the regrets with which he is preoccupied return: "Softened regrets they might be, teaching me what I had failed to learn when my younger life was all before me, but not the less regrets. 'Oh Trot,' I seemed to hear my aunt say once more; and I understood her better now—'Blind, blind, blind!' " The irony is clear: David is quite as blind in his new pride as he had ever been. He is so proud, in fact, that he reaffirms his determination to repress his feelings for Agnes and merely "cherishes his fancies." By the end of his first post-recovery interview with Agnes it is apparent that David is relapsing into his old behavior, as though the consciousness of the lesson is subverting its effectiveness.

David is, at this point, a "model penitent." The irony in the model prison really reflects David's absurdity, rather than, as Q. D. Leavis suggests, the absurdity of the prisoners. The responses of Littimer and Heep to Creakle's catechism are strongly reminiscent of David's thoughts during his Dark Night. "I see my follies now, sir," says Heep, "that's what makes me comfortable"; "I see my follies now," echoes Littimer. These proclamations are, in fact, caricatures of David's earlier words:

> In the beginning of the change that gradually worked in me, when I tried to get a better understanding of myself and be a better man, I did glance, through some indefinite probation, to a period when I might possibly hope to cancel the mistaken past, and to be so blessed as to marry her [Agnes]. . . . [But] the time was past. I had let it go by, and had deservedly lost her.

As Heep's dialogue with Creakle continues, the ironies become stronger:

> "You are quite changed?" said Mr. Creakle.
> "Oh dear, yes, sir!" cried this hopeful penitent.
> "You wouldn't relapse, if you were going out?"
> "Oh de-ar, no, sir!"

Of course the reader knows, as David knows, that prisoners "Twenty Seven and Twenty Eight [are] perfectly consistent and unchanged." The reader, by now, should also see the incompleteness of David's development.

David's problem throughout has been his egocentricity. In his youth it was unconscious—David failed to see the implications of his thoughts and actions. This egocentricity was replaced, however, by one of excessive consciousness. Self-analysis, self-discipline, self-sacrifice—in all these the emphasis is on *self*. What had saved David earlier, and what he needs now, is a faith in himself which would preclude unhealthy introspection. Recall Agnes's letter, quoted above: "she gave me no advice; she urged no duty on me; she only told me, in her fervent manner, what her trust in me was."

This is the faith in himself that David needs. He has gained the necessary "healthy self-awareness," but he has gone too far, and is still preoccupied with himself. The visit to Creakle's prison, then, serves a special function here, for the incident is comic, and comedy is precisely what David needs to break the spell of his over-seriousness. As he remarks to Traddles, "Perhaps it's a good thing . . . to have an unsound Hobby ridden hard; for it's the sooner ridden to death." It is time now for David to stop riding the "Hobby" of his own repentance.

It is important, however, that David not make this connection, for he is already paralyzed by his surfeit of consciousness. Quite properly, his recovery now is gradual, and his introspection fades slowly:

> At least once a week, and sometimes oftener, I rode over there [to Agnes], and passed the evening. I usually rode back at night; for the old unhappy sense was always hovering about me now—most sorrowfully when I left her—and I was glad to be up and out, rather than wandering over the past in weary wakefulness or miserable dreams. I wore away the longest part of many wild sad nights, in those rides; reviving, as I went, the thoughts that had occupied me in my long absence.
>
> Or, if I were to say rather that I listened to the echoes of those thoughts, I should better express the truth. They spoke to me from afar off.

These horseback rides have a metaphoric identity with David's Hobby-riding, and the Hobby is wearing out. At Christmastime—the season of grace—David takes his final horseback ride to Agnes, for hereafter he will ride with her, not alone. He rides his Hobby one last time, too. His aunt has told him that Agnes is to be married soon, and noble, self-sacrificing David is riding to congratulate her. Agnes, of course, bursts into tears—partly for David's blindness, and partly, I think, for the ease with which he seems able to give her up. But here the Hobby dies. Witnessing the pain he has caused Agnes, David forgets all his resolutions and vows, caring more for the feelings of another than for himself, and declares his love.

David's recovery is finally complete, for in Agnes's love he finds the grace that brings the true penitent to salvation. Losing himself to find himself, David is no longer preoccupied with the tag lines of his lessons; he has learned the deeper meaning behind them. In doing so, he becomes the novel's most interesting, and most successful, penitent.

# David Sees "Himself" in the Mirror

*Barry Westburg*

Many critics who discuss growth, crisis, and conversion in Dickens's novels choose to focus on explicitly "moral" themes, such as that of the "undisciplined heart" in *Copperfield*, to the exlusion of what might be called the growth of consciousness, of which overt moral changes are the often rather sententiously announced outcome. Accordingly, when a critic with moral preoccupations looks for "change of heart" in Dickens's novels, he usually looks at adult crises and finds some rather crude stereotyped reversals and "gap[s] between the flow of events and the moral action." If one's notions of moral change in novels are derived from the practices of George Eliot, evidently psychomimetic, then Dickens's practices are likely to seem unsatisfying and to demand some apologetics. But even if one manages to find an almost Eliot-like subtlety (as Gwendolyn B. Needham seems to do) in the "recognition" that characters like David Copperfield come to, emphasis on moral growth per se can lead to neglect of the childhood crises of consciousness that are Dickens's greatest achievements in imaginary psychology. These early crises establish postures of the self that play important parts in future development and influence moral growth itself. Some themes like the disciplining of the heart—the narrator's explicit discussion of it being one of the most forgettable parts of *Copperfield*—need to be seen as almost epiphenomena, or as generalized approximations to deeper imaginative concerns that reveal themselves persistently from the very first.

*Copperfield* is a drama of memory, but it is also a drama of the imagination. Imagination and memory are intimately connected in growth, transforming the present and helping to create the future. Since Dickens treats of imagination and memory for the most part as functions—remembering and imagining as differential functions—they are not always visible as discrete psychic states. We have seen how memory can contaminate perception (how the activity of remembering can intermittently displace that of perceiving). Similarly, the imagination contaminates perception. This happens most frequently at moments of crisis; for it seems part of the point of Dickens's imaginary psychology to center on moments at which ordinary conceptions of mental faculties prove unhelpful or lead to ambiguities for the reader who tries to think with them. Thus, as usual, Dickens chooses to exploit occasions where there is a certain opportunity for free construction. And, in general, in accord with this project of constructing an imaginary psychology, Dickens forecloses on the possibility of thinking about psychic growth with simple equations or structures in mind. For instance, the "theory of memory" is quite complex enough to dispel any simplistic notion that remembering as such is nondevelopmental. True enough, certain kinds of remembering can retard growth and turn the personality to stone, but others can foster growth in important ways. The same is true of imagination. Imagination helps David to deal with crisis, but it also offers him a questionable new identity. Crisis generates a symbolic thinking that is quite different from remembering but which can offer equally seductive pleasures, so that the initiate can merely exchange one static way of being for another. The pleasures of the symbol (or, if one prefers, more generally, the pleasures of the imagination) are bound up with the problem of narcissism, and Dickens explores narcissism as an essential obstacle to personal relationships.

Murdstone, who terrorizes with Order the sweet confusion of Blunderstone Rookery, intrudes into David's life and precipitates his first genuine identity crisis. The timeless pleasures of childhood thereupon come to be replaced by the cruel necessities of living in time, and the boy must change or go under. The most important episode of this crisis begins when David, upon provocation, bites Murdstone's hand, and is beaten viciously and confined to his room. In response to an evil action, he (with a vitality usually found only in the Dickens child) commits one in return. Violence begins by imitating violence. Oliver Twist's rage at Noah Claypole was a temporary and unique instance of rebellion and vanished like clouds after a storm, but David's rebellion put him permanently into a new position and a new frame of mind. Both boys have to leave the country and go to the city as a result of rebellion, a significant pattern; but in David we see the resulting mental adjustment that begins at the moment of rebellion itself. Here is part of the scene:

> He beat me . . . as if he would have beaten me to death. Above all the noise we made, I heard them running up the stairs, and crying out—I heard my mother crying out—and Peggotty. Then he was gone; and the door was locked outside; and I was lying, fevered and hot, and torn, and sore, and raging in my puny way, upon the floor.
>
> How well I recollect, when I became quiet, what an unnatural stillness seemed to reign through the whole house! How well I remember, when my smart and passion began to cool, how wicked I began to feel.
>
> I sat listening for a long while, but there was not a sound. I crawled up from the floor, and saw my face in the glass, so swollen, red, and ugly that it almost frightened me. My stripes were sore and stiff, and made me cry afresh, when I moved; but they were nothing to the guilt I felt. It lay heavier on my breast than if I had been a most atrocious criminal. . . .
>
> Long after it was dark I sat there. . . . I undressed, and went to bed; and there, I began to wonder fearfully what would be done to me. Whether it was a criminal act that I had committed? . . . Whether I was at all in danger of being hanged?

The scene begins with the body as its "theme." In Dickens's novels the body is frequently (as in the developmental novels, and, with Esther, in *Bleak House*) discovered in pain, imprisonment, and guilt—that is, by and as limitation. Here the discovery of the body is connected with certain imaginative steps. First we note that in the symmetry of David's counter-action against Murdstone he is in a way testing his sense of a crude analogy: that Murdstone, the embodiment of otherness, is like him in that he can be hurt, too. Rousseau, Edmund Gosse, and many others have testified to the importance of the lesson that one's father is not a god. But if Murdstone is mortal, so, emphatically, is David. He is beaten further "as if he would have beaten me to death." Thanks to the unequal distribution of power, some actions do not evoke opposite and equal reactions. This failure on a purely physical level is something that many of Dickens's heroes seem to experience, a fact which transforms their imaginative life as they seek more effective means of response on higher levels. This scene occurs, incidentally, in David's bedroom; he is at the very center of shelter and yet can still be harmed by a force that cannot be walled out, and which can, by its intrusion, turn the house [and self] inside out, so that the shelter becomes a prison.

David's pain at first identifies his body with the self at "the center," but as soon as the body is felt from the inside the next step is to see the body from the outside, just as the child's house was first known from within and then was seen in an alienated vision from without. Dickens's use of a mirror in this scene has almost exactly the meaning of Charlotte Brontë's use of one in the very similar scene, published in 1847, in which Jane Eyre, because she lashed back at her tormentor, is imprisoned in the "red room." This is the way Brontë presents the moment:

> Alas! . . . no jail was ever more secure. Returning, I had to cross before the looking-glass; my fascinated glance involuntarily explored the depth it revealed. All looked colder and darker in that visionary hollow than in reality: and the strange little figure there gazing at me, with a white face and arms specking the gloom, and glittering eyes of fear moving where all else was still, had the effect of a real spirit.

David, as well, momentarily sees himself as almost an alien being: "My face in the glass, so swollen, red, and ugly that it almost frightened me." But the important step is the subsequent accommodation of the mirror, the recognition that that particular other is really one-self. Jacques Lacan, in his article on *le stade du miroir,* emphasizes the significance of this experience for infants—real infants. "L'assomption jubilatoire de son image spéculaire par l'être encore plongé dans l'impuissance motrice et la dépendance du nourrissage qu'est le petit homme à ce stade *infans,* nous paraîtra dès lor manifester en une situation exemplaire la matrice symbolique où le *je* se précipite en une forme primordiale, avant qu'il ne s'objective dans la dialectique de l'identification à l'autre et que le langage ne lui restitue dans l'universel sa fonction de sujet." [This jubilant assumption of his specular image by the child at the *infans* stage, still sunk in his motor incapacity and nursling dependence, would seem to exhibit in an exemplary situation the symbolic matrix in which the *I* is precipitated in a primordial form, before it is objectified in the dialectic of identification with the other, and before language restores to it, in the universal, its function as subject.] Lacan goes on to say that "le point important est que cette forme situe l'instance du *moi,* dès avant sa détermination sociale, dans une *ligne de fiction*" (my italics) [the important point is that this form situates the agency of the ego, before its social determination, in a fictional direction] (from Lacan, *Ecrits: A Selection,* trans. Alan Sheridan. New York & London: W. W. Norton, 1977).

Dickens and Brontë offer the mirror-perspective to their children precisely at an early moment of suffering and "impuissance motrice." Both writers exploit the mirror experience fully and offer it as symbolic of a step in the development of the self—a self seen as growing in moments of imaginative transcendence.

The scene in *Copperfield,* after revealing the discovery of the body and the discovery of the complex, self-conscious self, leads to further effects, which can be compared with the effect on Oliver Twist of reading the Newgate Calendar. Bodily punishment by others leads to mental self-punishment. As David says, the bodily suffering is "nothing" to the guilt he feels. This remark distances the body from the deeper self which now feels a pain qualitatively different from that of the body. And just as David's awakened imagination now explores the parts of the house where he cannot be, so does this imagination explore for the first time the imaginative world of the others. By doing so he does not merely await judgment and definition by them, he unconsciously attempts to anticipate them and, in a way, to punish himself in advance in his imagination. He makes a rudimentary attempt at self-evaluation using the limited terms adults have given him; naturally these terms have a simplistic, either-or character to them. Was it "a criminal act that I had committed?" Was I "at all in danger of being hanged?" In his attempt at evaluation David has to go beyond his primitive stance in a new way by exploring the objective role of criminal; furthermore, he can do this only by trying to think the thoughts of the judge as well. Even to begin to think of himself as an "atrocious criminal," as he does, is to accept the supposed judgment of Murdstone, is to be Murdstone for himself. Before, David had been in no need of any justification; now he demonstrates that he feels the mithradatic necessity of internalizing Murdstone's probable notions, of standing apart within himself and seeing as provisionally real the David whom he imagines Murdstone has imagined. Imitating authority is perhaps the necessary preliminary to becoming one's own authority; if the process is successful, David can eventually (as an autobiographer, for instance) substitute his own judgments for those of the judges.

Returning to the mirror-event itself, we can see how the mirrors in *Copperfield* suggest that the hero functions as a kind of imaginative tool for exploring the limits of the artistic imagination. *Copperfield* is concerned with exploring the power of symbols, especially their role in self-development, and does this in an "erotic" context. That is, the narcissism of symbol-using is examined as an alternative to intimate human relationships.

In this sense the novel is about aesthetic education far more than about "erotic" education, though the two are of course linked. Only indirectly is it about "disciplining" David's heart, a thesis which once gained its authority (I think) from the widespread impression that, though David is ostensibly a famous writer, we actually hear next to nothing about his works. It is precisely this apparent absence of the "work" that misleads many readers into believing that the novel is about something more down-to-earth than aestheticism and artists. Need we be reminded that *Copperfield* itself is offered as the work written by David?

Six times, in similar and momentous circumstances, David sees himself in the mirror. Now the mirror is not simply an image, and in this I see its importance for Dickens's novel—for any aestheticist novel, perhaps. To the extent that it is an image, it comes as close as possible to imaging pure structure. The simplest of all structures is inherent in repetition, and the mirror is a static image of repetition. Further, it exists to frame or contain other images: it *images* (v. t.) or presents other images, and thus is the purest image we can conceive of for presenting the notion of image as such. In a novel, then, a mirror is not necessarily on the same level as other images; it tends to be estranged from everything else. To put a mirror into a novel—and novels have themselves been likened to mirrors, of course—is to create what in the passage from *Jane Eyre* is called a "visionary hollow," a hole in the work, which is imageless and yet which is also a form of *meta*-image in that it comments recursively on itself and upon the other images around it. Empty and irreal, the mirror can nevertheless derealize surrounding images, can put in question their reality. It foregrounds itself. Thus, whenever a novel—especially a first-person, reflexive novel—uses mirrors insistently, it is commenting on itself, saying something it cannot say with other images, the rest of which (except those expressing the phenomenon of mirroring: doubles, shadows, reflections in water, plot redoublements, and the like) cannot be so readily about themselves and still be themselves at the same time. In reflecting suffering and love (the singular and plural aspects of real life) the mirror draws attention to its own power and thus to the power of the symbol over real life.

Consider further Jacques Lacan's claim that a real infant reaches a crucial stage of development when, at around six months of age, it suddenly and joyfully recognizes itself in the mirror; when, thereupon, "le *je* se précipite en une forme primordiale." Maurice Merleau-Ponty, in his essay "The Child's Relations with Others," substantiates this insight by drawing on objective psychological studies and developing a detailed theory of what he calls, on the symbolic level, "l'image spéculaire," and on the literal, "l'image du miroir." Understanding these images evidently is central to understanding the growth of the real person. Dickens the novelist leads us through a gallery of mirrors, and they also are used, these seemingly humble images, to mark stages on life's way, to punctuate crucial moments for consciousness, as David moves from childhood simplicities to adulthood complexities.

In Dickens's use of mirrors, however, there is an emphasis on a circumstance not accounted for by Lacan or Merleau-Ponty. This emphasis is a clue to the way an imaginary consciousness can differ from a real one. To begin with, we cannot fully understand the imaginary consciousness created in *Copperfield* by using the basic "self / other" contrast of the psychologists. According to Merleau-Ponty, a real, ordinary child is shown the mirror by another person, can compare the person beside him with the image of that person in the mirror, and can then easily correlate the leftover image there with himself, so as to begin to learn about his own separateness, to discover his own space. There is no mystery in this very simple imaginative act. But in literary examples of mirror-gazing, a different process is usually involved, as the writings of Dickens, Charlotte Brontë, Poe, Mallarmé, Sartre, and others testify. The fictive initiate discovers his mirror-image all by himself: therefore in a much more radically imaginative and mysterious act. Also, the typically fictional form of the mirror-experience is essentially negative, while real children supposedly react to the encounter happily (Lacan speaks of "jubilation"), and it is invariably beneficial to their growth. For normal people the mirror seems, indeed, to initiate symbolic activity, along with the awareness that it is only symbolic activity. But many artists seem to resent or even fear that image, perhaps because it cannot, for them, be so easily reduced to mere image and then generally ignored, as we are told is the normal case. Otto Rank has commented on the frequency with which "autoscopic" experiences occur for artists in their lives and in their art, as if the mirror-image of the self haunts artists as it haunted primitive man. Understandably, if there is a marked difference in this one respect between the experiences of artists and those of ordinary people, then one might expect the difference between fictive characters and ordinary people to be every bit as great.

Accordingly, much more useful than the self / other distinction for exploring mirrors in art is the subjective / objective polarity used by Jean-Paul Sartre in his meditations on artists who have had to wrestle with the paradoxes of narcissism. It takes a thief to catch a thief; Sartre, discussing Flaubert and *Madame Bovary*, speaks with precise abstraction of the "objectification of the subjective" as a tendency of *homo faber*. Further, he speaks of "the moving unity of subjectivity and objectivity, those cardinal determinants of activity." Dickens's several accounts of growing up (especially in *Copperfield* and *Great Expectations*) could be described as explorations of the ways that characters live through the subjective phase of growth, with its intermittent egocentric solitude (subjectivity), punctuated by times of thing-like manipulation by others (objectivity), so as eventually to accomplish their successful "objectification." Objectification for the narrator of *Copperfield* is envisaged, first, as the creation of a positive, definitive, even redemptive work of art. He seeks a form of personal knowledge and potency as well as an intimate communion with others, both to be made possible by art. Whether he can achieve either or both of these things is a central question in the novel. If, as Robert Langbaum says, "The whole conscious concern with objectivity as a *problem,* as something to be achieved, is . . . specifically romantic," then here Dickens again shows his affinity with the "modern tradition" of Romanticism. Substitute Sartre's "objectification" for Langbaum's "objectivity" and we have the appropriate terms. David's life can be described as a prolonged oscillation between the poles of subjectivity and objectivity, both of which are prior to any true objectification. Were this final stage attainable, interaction between self and other would pass beyond the subjectivity / objectivity oscillation altogether (that oscillation being essentially narcissistic, the drama of a persons' relations with himself and his imaginings), and the hero would reach what Merleau-Ponty and many others see as the goal of maturity: a true non-narcissistic communication. This would not be the delicious commingling of identities that many lovers value, but rather a meeting with others as other. Other people would not serve as mere backdrops for the hero's projections of his own wishes, nor would they offer him the chance to copy, on the slate of his own bemused soul, their perhaps alien ways.

Mirrors in *Copperfield* often suggest both the advantages and the dangers of self-awareness; mirrors provide orientation, but they can also come between oneself and others, causing communicative, even erotic, distortion. Though his hero does not develop adequately, Dickens at least shows with his mirrorings that he has begun to understand why David cannot be imagined into maturity. The central moment of the first crisis, as we have seen, produces the mirror image. The conflict with Murdstone began because David was not learning things fast enough (reading, Latin grammar, sums), but the conflict itself takes education to a much deeper level than before. In this "spot of time," Dickens penetrates to what, for a real child, would have been a crisis of early infancy—when, according to Merleau-Ponty, the most important issue is "consciousness of one's own body and the specular image." Dickens shows us, as in a "time-warp," a moment of transformation, when infantile unity is replaced (through bodily pain and specular scrutiny) by a new sense of distance, boundary, perspective; a split in the world that is also a split in the self. David must now "lie a long way off" from his mother; the mirror, which at first shows him himself as a stranger, records this decentering. The crisis brings about a qualitative leap in development—a veritable conversion of quantity to quality.

But decentering does not produce for David, as it supposedly does for real children, a true, objective view of himself. One can guess from David's excessive insistence on his guilt feelings that his rivalry with Murdstone has taken, if anything, an even more deeply subjective form. While he learns the lesson taught him by Murdstone and the mirror at one level—as is evident in some of his later facility in handling mirrors—at another level emerges the threat of a neurotic stasis and narcissism. The whole book, his whole life, seems to whirl around this moment, and the time-stoppage is reflected even in the repetitive structure of the novel, an appropriate formal analogue to the memorial circularities and obsessions of both child and adult Copperfield. (Prior to this crisis David had seen a mirror, though Dickens does not have him look into it. But according to one of my students, Elizabeth A. Burns, the event does qualify as a seventh instance of Dickens's critical use of mirrors in *Copperfield*. David's first impressions of the Peggotty household at Yarmouth include a view of the bedroom he will occupy at "the stern of the vessel." "It was the completest and most desirable bedroom ever seen . . . with a little window, where the rudder used to go through; and a little looking-glass, just the right height for me, nailed against the wall, and framed with oyster-shells. . . . " The passage is quite resonant when thought of in proximity both with David's first and with his final mirror vision, the latter also at Yarmouth, involving shipwreck and the like. In both of the earlier passages mirrors and windows in bedrooms are side by side, while in the later one mirror and window, again in a bedroom, merge into one and the same image.)

According to Merleau-Ponty, for real children, "jealousy is overcome thanks to the constitution of a scheme of past-present-future. In effect jealousy in [a] subject consists in a rigid attachment to his present—that is, to the situation . . . which was hitherto his own." To study the profound role of memory and imagination in this novel is to recognize the importance of this early event involving the body, a father who is less a real person than an image out of projective fantasy, and the mirror. Recapture of the original childhood idyll, in an involuntary memory that distorts the objective "scheme of past-present-future" by coming forward to possess the present, is not at all rewarding, because the hard times of childhood come along with the good ones. Memorial regression would be fortunate indeed if only the eternally recurring childhood, so supple at insinuating itself into adult consciousness as pure perception, did not appear thus dyadic.

When he begins his autobiography David is a celebrated author and supposedly a mature man, but he is haunted by this dyadic childhood in which good and evil coexist as if inseparable, though he wants to keep the good for himself and precipitate out the memory of evil, to make sure that the evil is "other." He wants to remember at will only the good times, but, like the hero of *The Haunted Man,* he cannot be selective. Unlike Dickens, who abandoned a real to write a fictional autobiography, David intends to use his sincerest art (the supposedly mimetic art that shows everything, as in a mirror) to complete his maturation and to orient himself to both art and love. He begins his self-researches by positing two deceptive alternatives: "Whether I shall turn out to be the hero of my own life, or whether that station will be held by anybody else." In short, am I self-made or made by others? Either alternative, if embraced fully, amounts to the same thing, which reflects a basic narcissism (solipsism and monism) not uncommon in artists who attempt autobiography. In both instances other people would have to be seen as either ciphers (mere phenomena) or symbols. In the former case (David Hero) the other would be internalized, while in the latter (David as Prisoner of Grace) the self would evaporate, and action and motive would be thrust upon symbolically dominant others, who can do anything, especially what the hero secretly most wishes to do. A realist critic of this behavior would say that David invents those others, whether they seem potent or vacuous. But the very fact that David begins by posing that truly existential question about his life means that he will direct his consciousness toward a specific end, and thus reduce the richness of his avowedly global memory in doing so. Even though he is not able consistently to maintain this posture, his autobiography will still be every bit as fictive as Dickens's pseudo-autobiographical novel. Without knowing it, David is writing a novel about his life, hopefully to create himself as his own hero, independent of others' definitions of him. This is one sense in which *Copperfield,* while appearing to be about mutual love and exchanges of nurture, is actually about narcissism and its related aestheticism.

David discovers his problematic objectivity while locked in his room confronting a stranger in his mirror; but the isolation from the world and the human community has also its corresponding subjective moment, so that we see for David a two-way split—from the world and also within himself. As early as *Sketches by Boz* ("A Visit to Newgate") Dickens viewed imprisonment as a pyschological disturbance; later he always used it as an occasion for mental development or at least transformation. During David's imprisonment in his room he endures a subjective, solitary time ("the uncertain pace of the hours") and the sense of foreground-background reversal. He hears doors closing, footsteps, voices merely as voices—all the normally unperceived sounds. During this seemingly interminable imprisonment his personal world is a negative of the commonly shared one. It is as if he had passed through the looking-glass like Alice. He is thus complex, with an inside and an outside. But he finds his freedom in the eye, in the objective adult organ that enables him to explore his painfully limited body in the mirror. After all, he can direct his gaze, but he cannot close his ears. When he accepts the image there as somehow also himself, the mirror becomes a tool. This is use of metaphor: taking the emanation, his fictive projection, a ghost on the glass, as a reality. And temporarily this is an aestheticist stance that diminishes the hero, for himself, to the sum of his surfaces.

The second time David sees himself in the mirror is that "memorable birthday" when he learns of his mother's death, and, as he says, feels "like an orphan in the wide world." This is the first of four deaths that mark important stages in his life (Dora's, Ham's, and Steerforth's are the others). After exhausting his first tears, David says:

> I stood upon a chair when I was left alone, and looked into the glass to see how red my eyes were, and how sorrowful my face. . . . I am sensible of having felt that a dignity attached to me among the rest of the boys, and that I was important in my affliction. . . . I remember that this importance was a kind of satisfaction to me, when I walked in the playground. . . . When I saw them glancing at me out of the windows, as they went up to their classes, I felt distinguished, and looked more melancholy, and walked slower.

He looks to confirm his devastation; he has come far from that first accidental glimpse. The self-image has precedence over emotion. Instead of dwelling on the purity of reaction, Dickens shows how real suffering soon gives way to the public gesture. David tries to see himself as others will see him and models his imagined exterior for them. At the end of this scene David is placed (with Dickens's usual finesse) on the outside of the school looking in, while the others are inside looking out. During the first crisis while hiding from the imagined gaze of children playing outside his house, David felt segregation from others. Now he exhibits himself, asking that his suffering (birthday suffering, no less) be seen as his isolating, distinguishing feature. Exhibitionism is no less immature and subjective than hiding, though, and it is also a subtler alienation.

In most narratives of growing up there is at least one scene in which the hero, often with the aid of potions or dreams, journeys into strange regions of experience; this is important to the logic of such narrative, in that it tests perceptual norms and disrupts some of them enough to create new orientation. David, during his "first dissipation," accordingly befuddles himself with drink and strong tobacco:

> Somebody was leaning out of my bedroom window, refreshing his forehead against the cool stone of the parapet, and feeling the air upon his face. It was myself. I was addressing myself as "Copperfield," and saying, "Why did you try to smoke? You might have known you couldn't do it." Now, somebody was unsteadily contemplating his features in the looking-glass. That was I too. I was very pale in the looking-glass; my eyes had a vacant appearance; and my hair—only my hair, nothing else—looked drunk.

Dickens then describes drunken confusions of time and space; for example, "I stepped at once out of the box-door [of the theatre] into my bedroom." (In the comparable "Circe" episode of *Ulysses*, Mr. Bloom observes that "drunks cover distance double quick.") Here part of David is Admonisher, part is Strayed Reveller, and there is perspective within perspective of him. Somebody is in the glass, somebody sees that somebody, and somebody sees that seeing; and the narrator's own vision subtends all this. Thus Dickens makes it explicit once again that point of view is an issue, that he is exploring aesthesis in a general sense. David has been trying to play the role of man-about-town for Steerforth and friends (one of whom, by the way, "always spoke of himself indefinitely, as 'a man,' and seldom or never in the first person singular"). In an alternating subjectivity and objectivity, David keeps losing and finding himself in the mirror, which seems also to take on a new function. It offers a critical view that almost is that of a real other person. Its illusory depth now, in the midst of this extreme identity diffusion, offers what must pass for truth. "I was very pale." Actually the mirror has been doing this all along, but in different contexts, so that what it is able to tell David is each time different. It earlier taught him about his body and the need for hiding; then it taught him the possibility of disguise and deception; but now it begins to suggest that it can turn against him and offer him a coldly objective image that cannot be managed for deceptive purposes. The mirror hints at the requirements of another who will not be fooled by images. The mirror is becoming a form of external knowing that is analogous to the perspective not of a superficial society but of a fellow human being.

In a passage canceled from the proof sheets of the novel, David is fully the self-bewitched fop, a fake eroticist, and the mirror for the last time offers genial criticism. Clearly, it serves to focus narcissist-eroticist ironies in the novel. David tries to use his image seductively but finds himself unable to integrate his outside (as he images it) with an inside that does not even seem to know what it means. "Sometimes I am persuaded [Miss Larkins] must be aware of [my attachment to her] on account of my agitation and the expression on my face when I meet her; then I look in the glass, and getting up that expression as nearly as I can, doubt it, and suspect it may not reveal what I mean." The gentle, humorous self-depreciation in this passage shows that the narcissistic use of the mirror and the body-image is becoming more difficult, especially in relation to a person who insists on being herself while overlooking her admirer.

When "Doady" falls in love with the childish, inadequate Dora, another abnormal state of mind ensues, just as when he had suffered from Murdstone, from his mother's death, and from the confusion of being disguised in drink. "Lost in blissful delirium," he listens to the girl's singing. "When Miss Murdstone took her into custody and led her away, she smiled and gave me her delicious hand. . . . I caught a view of myself in the mirror, looking perfectly imbecile and idiotic." This "objectivity" is still best understood as the narrator's hyperbolic self-criticism. But there is a greater than usual ironic distance: the narrator's presence comes to the fore, as he revives before himself, through memory aided by imagination, the earlier self which is now his *Seelenspiegel*. The mirror's mythic job is to tell the negative truth (as at the entrance to Dante's Purgatory), and so it begins to do, especially for that concerned, backward-looking narrator. But the hero, bright-fledged flaneur, whose cues are an imagined reflection in the eyes of others, persists in his folly of tight boots, at once bruising body to pleasure the Dandiacal Soul and sacrificing his real soul to the all-important exterior.

The last mirror in *Copperfield* appears during a most crucial period in David's development; the time when he is faced with a manhood crisis that corresponds to, and certainly is a thematic answer to, the childhood crisis initiated by Murdstone. The principal figure at this point in his life is Steerforth, who brings adult eroticism into temporary focus as Murdstone could never have done. David arrives at Yarmouth during the tempest (so emphatic as transformation symbol) that is about to destroy Steerforth.

Once again, in this admirable episode, the mirror is associated (as at the beginning) with pain, alienation, and death—and again the context is covertly erotic. Copperfield is in his hotel room, pacing nervously about: "I got up several times, and looked out; but could see nothing, except the reflection in the window-panes . . . of my own haggard face looking in at me from the black void." Dickens's use of reflection in this passage is significant, for it suggests interwoven narcissist-eroticist problems, and, more generally, it helps us to understand related identity questions that Dickens was exploring in mid-career. Jorge Borges says that "mirrors have something monstrous about them." The window as mirror appears now almost monstrously. The ordinarily clear relation between the indoors and outdoors becomes ambiguous, thus undermining our sense of David's safety, which might otherwise have been based on a feeling of the contrast between storm and the privileges of shelter. In this moment, the mirror becomes linked with the important network of images in the novel that are associated with houses. Dickens is a supreme poet and dreamer of buildings—for him (to transpose Heidegger's famous metaphor) houses are the language of being. In a continuing harmonics of open and closed dwelling-spaces Dickens elaborates the very process of becoming. This storm scene first hints at the interpenetration of a builded enclosure and an inhuman chaos, which, in terms of the personal crisis just beginning, symbolizes a deeper emergent ambiguity. For two interfused versions of identity figure here, and both are momentarily sustained as simultaneously valid: the clearly outlined self as derived from human relationships and the stress of community; and identity as self-derived (an isolated self which, by comparison with the communal, bounded one, is unbounded, chaotic, inhuman, faintly autochthonous). David is in a zero hour of the imagination: at this fork in the labyrinth of symbols he will choose either the path of mystification or that of lucidity. The one is narcissistic, leading by incessant circlings to a center of self which is illusory (and without circumference); the other leads into the community, where boundaries (as between the inside and outside, self and other) exist in support of identity. The narcissist takes mirror images and the images of other people as versions of himself, as symbolically potent. The ordinary consciousness takes such images not as powerful symbols but merely as images without much content, depth, or significance.

Dickens is evidently trying to imagine for David an unambiguous way out of the subjectivity / objectivity split, the narcissism, shown up to now. Since Steerforth, who has often been called, perhaps without too much thought about it, David's alter ego, is out there in mortal peril, David's "haggard" face, coming as if from out there, has in effect been substituted for Steerforth's. Dickens obviously suggests this; had he been a surrealist he would have shown Steerforth's face at the window. For supposedly David's identity is involved in Steerforth's fate, because the latter has selfishly abused Emily, the girl who had once been the object of David's own (infantile) erotic fantasy. From this point of view, Steerforth is a negative projection, after having served his earlier contrary purpose as a positive model for David. He lives out David's desire for aggressive adult sex and pays for it, leaving David with clean hands and innocent memories. The mirror-image serves to remind us of their symbolic association, their doubling.

But by using the window as yet another mirror in this scene, Dickens superimposes upon this projective drama another one of quite opposite meaning, in which Steerforth plays no role at all, certainly in which the Steerforth-David equation is questioned, and thereby all symbolic appropriations of others. In the projective drama "Steerforth" is looking in from outside, and David is symbolically a Steerforth, voyaging without really voyaging, from sin to punishment. But in what we might term the counterpoised realist drama, David is seeing himself in the act of seeing, or, rather, is looking at an image of himself looking inwards to himself. The makeshift mirror shows thus an image of David in the posture he has actually assumed; the image is quite literal, perfectly accurate; for the mirror-window does make it impossible for David to look out; in trying to look out, he must encounter his own simulacrum as another person might see it. The image signals to readers who have the quite natural tendency to construct symbolic equations and to perceive doublings everywhere (as the hero himself does) that David is not connected with Steerforth as alter ego. Indeed, it is precisely his tendency to think so which is related to his split within himself: he is unable to see others nonsymbolically as other and himself literally as himself. It is not quite clear at this point what additional act of imagination or what intrusion would help David grow up (into a literal-minded adult). I would venture Dickens is intimating that David must first see the mirror as mirror, and the image as image, before it can become the window it really must become. Looking-*at* rather than looking-*into* would reveal to him the banality, the emptiness of the mirror and the specular image. The mirror would show him that it showed him only himself, as a literal image that then could not further operate as an identity transformer. This would lead him to see that the mirror was the symbol of his predicament, had been his predicament, and that by seeing through the simultaneous literalness and fictiveness of the mirror, he could then look-*through* the window to others. Thus the mirror would teach that it teaches nothing: a considerable lesson.

Because, as his later behavior shows, he does not learn this lesson,

David does not grow up; he marries a mother-sister-angel named Agnes who is merely more symbolic baggage. The business at the end about inner changes and Agnes's influence can be seen as a great deal of mystification designed to obscure the fact that David does not essentially change and that Agnes's presence indicates he need not change: for it seems to be Dickens's point in this novel not only that artists write fictions, but that their lives are fictions they have written themselves, stocked with gratifying images they have created out of real people who so miraculously feel the sway of imagination that they allow themselves to be used as screens upon which the self-absorbed artist can project symbolic variants of himself.

But the mirror shows that this is only a pleasant fancy of artists; doubtless it reveals up to this point, in Dickens himself, a real faith in the power of imagination to generate its own satisfactory objects—never mind whether in life or in art. Poetic faith is a biographical matter of some interest, but probably we can only point to it without proving it. But in novels mirrors are monstrous. Dickens learned enough about them in *Copperfield*, perhaps, to spare himself having to write works as shocking as E. T. A. Hoffmann's nightmarish tales, or, even more appropriately, Dostoyevski's *The Double*, where the ultimate horror is the vision of one's own face everywhere. This horror derives from the sense that everybody else is symbolically a version of oneself.

In his preface to *Copperfield* Dickens says, "I am a fond parent to every child of my fancy, and . . . no one can ever love that family as dearly as I love them." The novel is, he says, his "favourite child." We can only guess what a test in aesthetic possibilities *Copperfield* was for Dickens, who no doubt left it behind him (if *Great Expectations* is any indication) as his own mirror-stage in his striving for identity as an artist and as a person. This is biographical speculation, but I think he saw the child-monster in the mirror of his art and saw his favorite child as that child could not see itself (since it is evidently others who complete seeing). David reveals his shortcomings when he repeats the assertion that "this manuscript is intended for no eyes but mine." This is a conventional way of establishing the sincerity of sentimental, self-conscious narrative. But it is also the mark of an artist (and perhaps Dickens was like this artist) who wishes to define himself in bypassing—or re-creating—other people, an artist who will not venture himself, for to do so means simultaneously to abandon his own solipsistic distinctiveness and to admit the separateness and uniqueness of others. As Dickens later concluded, this is far from complete *confession*, which he came to see (in *Great Expectations*) as unsentimental, non-narcissistic, and formally ruthless.

# Remembrances of Death Past and Future: A Reading of *David Copperfield*

*Robert E. Lougy*

> *"I suppose history never lies, does it?" said Mr. Dick, with a gleam of hope.*
> *"Oh dear, no, sir!" I replied, most decisively. I was ingenuous and young, and I thought so.*
>
> *David Copperfield*

If enclosure within the silence of one's own mind is the particular form of madness that Dickens identifies in the mad gentleman and, later, in Steerforth's mother, there is another form of madness that also haunted the nineteenth-century artist, that of Arnold's Empedocles, wandering for eternity as a naked, restless mind, trapped in a prison of selfhood and separated forever from the world about him. This is the image of Childe Roland and Tennyson's Merlin as well; it is also the image of King Charles, haunting the psychic spaces of both Mr. Dick and the novel's hero. On the title page there is a dreaming or meditating infant in the center of the illustration; he appears to be both the creator and the prisoner of the structured chaos around him. In his dreams he is the child playing near the crib and the child who has imaginatively tamed death by converting the grave and tombstone into a make-believe coach. But, as we follow the illustration, we see that this child—the artist in the midst of his own created images—also appears to be an old man being led to the grave and, finally, he who lies in the grave. Like this child, David too is an artist surrounded by his own created

---

From *Dickens Studies Annual* 6 (1976). 

images, but his journey stops short of the grave and is resolved in such a way that he can tell his tale.

There is, however, another artist in *Copperfield* who is haunted by images, and his Memorial, unlike David's, remains unfinished. I am, of course, speaking of Mr. Dick. A descendant of the long tradition in Western literature of the fool as saint and the madman as sage, he is also the Romantic artist, the man haunted by images that come to him out of the past and prevent the completion of his creation, whether the work be Mr. Dick's Memorial, Wordsworth's *The Recluse,* Coleridge's *Biographia Literaria,* or Keats's "Hyperion." Like the Romantic artist, Mr. Dick still possesses the spontaneity and joyous freedom of childhood: "How often have I seen him, intent upon a match of marbles or peg-top, looking on with a face of unutterable interest, and hardly breathing at the critical times! . . . How many winter days have I seen him, standing blue-nosed, in the snow and east wind, looking at the boys going down the long slide, and clapping his worsted gloves in rapture!"

The Romantic artist, however, is not a child, but rather a man who has that capacity Coleridge identified in Wordsworth, the capacity to "carry on the feelings of childhood into the powers of manhood; to combine the child's sense of wonder and novelty with the appearances, which every day for perhaps forty years had rendered familiar." It is this same ability that David rightfully identifies in himself: "I believe the power of observation in numbers of very young children to be quite wonderful for its closeness and accuracy. Indeed, I think that most grown men who are remarkable in this respect, may with greater propriety be said not to have lost the faculty, than to have acquired it; the rather, as I generally observe such men to retain a certain freshness, and gentleness, and capacity for being pleased, which are also an inheritance they have preserved from their childhood."

If Mr. Dick is mad, his madness or unreason is radically different from that which finally encloses Mrs. Steerforth. While her madness imprisons her within a dominant will that has gone astray and has turned back upon itself to rend and immobilize, Mr. Dick's madness protects and comforts him. Maintaining him in a state of grace in a world without God, it enables him to remain innocent and wise and, through his actions, to define the limits of reason and to transcend those limits: " 'A poor fellow with a craze, sir,' said Mr. Dick, 'a simpleton, a weak-minded person—present company, you know!' striking himself again, 'may do what wonderful people may not do. I'll bring them [Dr. Strong and Annie] together, boy. They'll not mind what *I* do, if it's wrong. I'm only Mr. Dick. And who minds Dick? Whoo!' He blew a slight, contemptuous breath, as if he blew himself away."

King Charles's image causes Mr. Dick to doubt historical time with its clear delineation of the past and present, and, as David himself comes to realize, Mr. Dick's intuition is correct: history is a lie, a fiction creating a duration with continuity and coherence, telling us of a past in which the buried images of yesterday do not intrude upon the consciousness of the living.

As Betsey Trotwood suggests, Mr. Dick's struggle arises from a profound disturbance within himself created by the clash of the ideal with the real, between the love and compassion that should exist and the unkindness and cruelty he knows from experience do exist: " 'That's [King Charles's image] his allegorical way of expressing it. He connects his illness with great disturbance and agitation, naturally, and that's the figure, or the simile, or whatever it's called, which he chooses to use. And why shouldn't he, if he thinks proper?' " She goes on to add, however, that " 'It's not a business-like way of speaking . . . nor a worldly way. I am aware of that; and that's the reason why I insist upon it, that there shan't be a word about it in his Memorial.' " The public fear of madness demands that madness be hidden, concealed within a wall of silence and anonymity that will protect the outside world from it, even though this world itself is, as Mr. Dick observes, "mad as Bedlam, boy!" Madness in the nineteenth-century novel is frequently viewed not as a contained disruption within the psychic spaces of the inflicted but as a perpetual threat to the moral, economic, and ethical foundations of society. As metaphor, it is often a moral rather than a medical judgment, the consequences of excessive sexuality (Rochester's wife in *Jane Eyre*) or debauchery (*Vanity Fair*'s Steyne family). And if madness is defined, in part, as either the willful or involuntary separation of an individual from the productive forces of society, then the cure for such madness would include the incorporation of the individual into productivity; therapy, consequently, must be directed toward such inclusion. If the transgression is too grievous and the violation too great, the individual is consigned to a state of nonexistence (confinement taken to its logical extreme), destined to suffer and to offer penance to a world that demands it, even while denying the penitent any hope of salvation or forgiveness. Once Emily runs away with Steerforth, for example, she virtually ceases to exist in the novel (except to allow Mr. Peggotty and Rosa Dartle to fulfill their various destinies). Indeed, in several scenes—the confrontation of Emily and Rosa Dartle, and the departure of the emigrants—Dickens has to undergo artistic contortions in order to keep Emily concealed and quiet.

The ship on which the Peggottys sail is one containing emigrating paupers and transported criminals, mutual transgressors against the state and society. The image of such a ship captured the consciousness of the nineteenth century in much the same way the *Narrenschiff* captured the mind of the Middle Ages. But this latter-day vessel promised to society-at-large not the isolation of its insane but the exclusion of its poor and its outlaws. To its passengers it offered a new world, yet one that could only remind them of a past they could hope neither to expiate nor to forget. In a new land that was at the same time a moral construct, they would be forced, if they wished to survive, to cultivate the very virtues (labor, economy, and thrift) that would have prevented their downfall in the first place.

These same virtues, however, that are reinforced by the threat of transportation are undermined or threatened by Mr. Dick's metaphor, for it calls into being that chaos and nothingness that are barely concealed by the public myths of fulfillment, by David's dreams of the "figure I was to make in life." Mr. Dick's metaphor is, finally, too threatening; if allowed to exist, it would throw into jeopardy not only those public virtues but also the meaning of David's journey that is established by the conclusion of the novel. The significance of Mr. Dick's Memorial lies precisely in the fact that it cannot be completed, only terminated. Its fulfillment is always ahead of it, in order to be true to itself, it must acknowledge, by its incompletion, those images that prevent its satisfactory conclusion. Like the Baker's Song [in *The Hunting of the Snark*], the only authentic completion of the Memorial would coincide with the conclusion of his life. But this, of course, could not be in *David Copperfield*. Thus it is that the intrusion of the demonic and its concomitant recognition of a reality to which reason is blind can be held off only at the cost of a silence that descends upon and envelops the artist. The final containment of King Charles's image is accomplished by the mindless copying of other people's words, an act antithetical to language and discourse: " 'But these writings, you know, that I speak of, are already drawn up and finished,' said Traddles, after a little consideration. 'Mr. Dick has nothing to do with them.' " This therapy does have its rewards: it puts shillings into Mr. Dick's pocket and, more importantly, it includes him within the world of productivity and consumption: "He earned by the following Saturday night ten shillings and nine pence; and never, while I live, shall I forget his going about to all the shops in the neighbourhood to change this treasure into sixpences, or his bringing them to my aunt arranged in the form of a heart upon a waiter, with tears of joy and pride in his eyes." Mr. Dick's initial frenetic activity—"he was like a man playing the kettledrums, and constantly divided his attention between the two"—

does not last, and the poise he finally attains seems to be a permanent one: "finding this (the division of his attention) confused and fatigued him, and having his copy before his eyes, he soon sat at it in an orderly businesslike manner, and postponed the Memorial until a more convenient time." The virtues of prudence and orderliness prevail, and we must assume that the "more convenient time" will be forever postponed, permanently consigned to the realm of the unbusinesslike and the unworldly. During the final pages of the novel we are again told of the success of this treatment: "My aunt informed me how he incessantly occupied himself in copying everything he could lay his hands on, and kept King Charles the First at a respectful distance by that semblance of employment."

Several complex impulses seem to be operating within Dickens's description of Mr. Dick's transformation. First of all, King Charles's head is not gotten rid of, only kept at "a respectful distance" by writing with which Mr. Dick "has nothing to do." His redemption must be perpetually earned by means of an activity that Melville perceived quite differently in "Bartleby the Scrivener." The activity in both cases is identical: what differs is the moral or ethical construction within which each is set. And yet Melville is neither more compassionate than Dickens nor more aware of the madness and death impulse that lie barely beneath the surface of society's structures of normalcy and sanity. When Dickens binds Mr. Dick to Ixion's wheel, he does so gently and with compassion; it is an act whose moral and humane impulses we have to recognize and respect, one that sincerely wishes to bestow happiness and a restored sense of purpose and identity upon Mr. Dick. But it is also an act that is an image of a dream or desire that Dickens shared with his age, the fulfillment of which exacts a certain price, namely, a departure by the end of the novel from what Mr. Dick was to what, given the impulses behind his transformation, he should have been. It is difficult to reconcile the Mr. Dick we see throughout most of the novel, an individual filled with gaiety, spontaneity, and a great capacity for love, with the one Betsey Trotwood describes late in the novel as being saved from "pining in monotonous restraint" by the mindless copying of other people's words. His "semblance of employment" is an extreme image of Marx's "alienated labor," and there is no indication in the novel that it helps to rid him of his unreason. What it does is to make unreason respectable by enclosing it within an activity whose alienation is evidenced in the choreography of the act itself—of Mr. Dick and King Charles kept apart and isolated by a work wholly disassociated from the one who performs it. Madness is not cured; it is simply given another name.

> *That in the face of which one has anxiety is characterized by the fact that what threatens it is* nowhere. *Anxiety "does not know" what that in the face of which it is anxious is. . . . Therefore that which threatens cannot bring itself close from a definite direction within what is close by; it is already "there," and yet nowhere; it is so close that it is oppressive and stifles one's breath, and yet it is nowhere.*
>
> M. Heidegger, *Being and Time*

> *I fell into a dull slumber before the fire, without losing my consciousness, either because of the uproar out of doors, or of the place in which I was. Both became overshadowed by a new and indefinable lethargy that bound me in my chair—my whole frame thrilled with objectless and unintelligible fear.*
>
> *David Copperfield*

In Mr. Dick, the artist-as-child is killed, assimilated within a social and ethical vision that cannot accommodate either idleness or the demonic, yet it is not too surprising that the demonic will arise again in the novel, for its creator's own life suggests that he too was demon-ridden. The profound dissonance between interiority and adventure within a world that cannot reflect or fulfill that interior finds its extreme example in Mr. Dick, almost as if Dickens perceived in Mr. Dick's destiny the redemption and the silence of his novel's hero, an artist haunted by images less easily dispelled, one whose memorial is less easily concluded. But if *David Copperfield* concludes by enclosing its hero within a series of images inadequate to the search he has been waging, this conclusion occurs only after one of the most significant struggles waged in nineteenth-century British fiction.

It seems to me that the supreme moment of the struggle takes place in the "Tempest" chapter (55). In it David confronts directly those image-ridden winds that compel him on his journey. The language of this chapter seems disproportionate at times to the narrative action—the account of the deaths of Ham and Steerforth occupies only the last several paragraphs of the chapter—until we realize that while these deaths are required and anticipated by the plot, they occupy a subordinate position within the chapter. The chapter moves primarily toward a recognition of his own death that David can no longer conceal or evade; it gathers within itself all those images that David has confronted during his solitary pilgrimage and reveals them with an almost visionary translucency. The chapter's very beginning suggests that the depth it touches lies beyond those that can be accounted for by the plot alone, even by events so momentous as the deaths of Ham and Steerforth: "I now approach an event in my life, so indelible, so awful, so bound by an infinite variety of ties to all that has preceded it in these pages, that, from the beginning of my narrative, I have seen it growing larger and larger as I advanced, like a great tower in a plain, and throwing its fore-cast shadow even on the incidents of my childish days."

Whatever it is that David now approaches, he realizes that the whole narrative has been shaped and defined by it, even when David returns to his "childish days," he returns to a landscape shadowed by images from it. It is not an event of which he speaks, for it cannot be isolated by time or placed within a duration whose continuity it helps to establish. On the contrary, it stands before David now and has always stood before him; even as he writes of it, it exists for him as something that keeps slipping out of the actual into dreams, and then back into the actual again. It is not elicited, but, like the Ancient Mariner's curse (one that similarly compels the Mariner to tell his tale), it comes forth unbeckoned and unwelcome: "For years after it occurred, I dreamed of it often. I have started up so vividly impressed by it, that its fury has yet seemed raging in my quiet room, in the still night. I dream of it sometimes, though at lengthened and uncertain intervals, to this hour. I have an association between it and a stormy wind, or the lightest mention of a sea-shore, as strong as any of which my mind is conscious. As plainly as I behold what happened, I will try to write it down. I do not recall it, but see it done; for it happens again before me."

In its almost surreal rendering of nightmare, horror, and anxiety, this chapter is reminiscent less of other nineteenth-century fiction than of the age's poetry, in particular of Browning's "Childe Roland to the Dark Tower Came," an account of a nightmare journey that resembles David's. David tells his tale in order to put together those pieces of the net that are still disconnected; he journeys forth through memory in order to find the thread that runs through the "I" whose tale he is telling. The particular terror of the "Tempest" lies in the fact that it not only threatens the success of the journey, but threatens its very validity. The storm that breaks over Yarmouth and the ocean that threatens to pull the structures of the town back into itself represent the potential triumph of formlessness over form, of death over life. They portend the victory of a consciousless force pulling all alien matter back into itself: "As the receding wave swept back with a hoarse roar, it seemed to scoop out deep caves in the beach, as if its purpose were to undermine the earth. . . . Undulating hills were changed to valleys, undulating valleys (with a solitary storm-bird sometimes skimming through them) were lifted up to hills; masses of water shivered and shook the beach with a booming sound; every shape tumultuously rolled on, as soon as made, to change its shape and place, and beat another shape and place away;

the ideal shore on the horizon, with its towers and buildings, rose and fell; the clouds fell fast and thick; I seemed to see a rending and upheaving of all nature."

Within this chapter, images come forth out of David's early childhood to haunt him and to create anxieties for which he cannot find a discernible object or an identifiable cause. In speaking of the impact that this experience still has for him—"its fury has yet seemed raging in my quiet room, in the still night"—David uses a metaphor that isolates and defines those memories whose echoes reverberate most strongly within this chapter, and in turn gather their resonances from it; the memories evoked by this episode are primarily those of protected spaces violated by disruptions from within and without, and of those of the night and darkness throwing the certainty and comfort of the day into doubt. Images, at times fragmented and broken, of memories that are called forth include those of David's revisiting of Peggotty's ship-home after his own home had been broken up, of listening to the wind and "fancying . . . that it moaned of those who were gone," of Little Em'ly's challenging of the sea and his own fear of death by drowning, of himself in his childhood bedroom fearful of the intrusion of his father's ghost. All these images, like the storm itself, come to David, carrying impulses that are still within him as he tells his story. The direction of this chapter and the energies that lie behind it are extremely complex. Part of its problem (by which I do not mean fault or weakness) arises from Dickens's own awareness that his creation is ultimately inaccessible. He writes it, gives it being, but still he seems to comprehend it only partially. Perhaps realizing his inability to account fully for the scene, he chooses instead to allow it to come forth in all its complexity and ambivalence.

Indications of the inadequate correlation between the novel's narrated plot and the resonances of this chapter are found quite early. We discover that David is exhausted, restless, and in a mood that has an intense hold over him: "I was very much depressed in spirits; very solitary; and felt an uneasiness in Ham's not being there, disproportionate to the occasion. I was seriously affected, without knowing how much, by late events; and my long exposure to the fierce wind had confused me. There was that jumble in my thoughts and recollections, that I had lost the clear arrangement of time and distance. . . . So to speak, there was in these respects a curious inattention in my mind. Yet it was busy, too, with all the remembrances the place naturally awakened; and they were particularly distinct and vivid." Confused and jumbled by his "long exposure to the fierce wind," David feels disoriented in time and space. He may not know or be able to identify the sources of his uneasiness, but he is able to identify what the sources are not—his language carefully modifies and qualifies his ex periences: his uneasiness was "disproportionate to the occasion," and whe he writes of his apprehension, he observes that "*I was persuaded* that I ha an apprehension of his returning from Lowestoft by sea, and being lost. His anxiety is such that he cannot dispel it; and, as when the boat-builde laughs at his concern for Ham's safety, his search for external sources c consolation fail. After failing to find reassurance, David retires to his roon and the description which follows is critical.

> The howl and the roar, the rattling of the doors and windows, the rumbling in the chimneys, the apparent rocking of the very house that sheltered me, and the prodigious tumult of the sea, were more fearful than in the morning. But there was now a great darkness besides; and that invested the storm with new terrors, real and fanciful.
>
> I could not eat, I could not sit still, I could not continue steadfast to anything. Something within me, faintly answering to the storm without, tossed up the depths of my memory and made a tumult in them. Yet, in all the hurry of my thoughts, wild running with the thundering sea,—the storm and my uneasiness regarding Ham were always in the foreground. . . .
>
> I fell into a dull slumber before the fire, without losing my consciousness, either of the uproar out of doors, or of the place in which I was. Both became overshadowed by a new and indefinable horror; and when I awoke—or rather when I shook off the lethargy that bound me in my chair—my whole frame thrilled with objectless and unintelligible fear.

These passages are among the greatest descriptions of dread, of nothingnes and death, to be found in nineteenth-century literature. Dickens obviousl does not have the vocabulary that Heidegger and Sartre have given to ou age, but, being Dickens, he does not need it. In any event, it is when th search for a cause proportionate to the mood ceases, when the narrato allows the horror and unintelligibility of the scene to define themselves that we see a language fully capable of carrying its own weight and makin its own connections. It is when "great darkness" descends over the her that we see the interior and exterior in a momentary poise or harmon ("something within me, faintly answering to the storm without"); th terrors that are invested upon the storm by the darkness arise from a violen shaking not only of "the very house that sheltered me," but of all thos conceptual structures and fond hopes that David has created for his pro tection and comfort. The fear that he experiences is "objectless and unintelligible"; it reveals David to himself with unparalleled clarity and prescience. And when the order and coherence within which he has protected the "I" of the tale collapse, David confronts directly and without evasion those images which, even still, he does not fully understand. The history of which David writes—indeed, the very reasons behind his writing—are shaped and compelled by this episode, one that stands both in front of him and behind him: "I have seen it growing larger and larger as I advanced, like a great tower in a plain, and throwing its fore-cast shadow even on the incidents of my childish days."

Those images that David has carried throughout, those that have agitated his memory like a restless wind—the lunatic's peering face and his father's grave-enshrouded image—reappear, this time becoming fused within David's imagination with his own self-reflected image: "I got up several times, and looked out; but could see nothing, except the reflection in the window-pane of the faint candle I had left burning, and of my own haggard face looking in at me from the black void." Unlike his earlier confrontations with these images, David can no longer evade their full significance or diminish the terror of their meaning by mystifying the past or by reshaping his memory in the service of forgetting. The ordered delineation between the past and the present, the interior and the exterior, life and death, break down; and the images of David, of the lunatic gentleman, and of David's father merge into an experience that speaks to David of "despondency and madness," nothingness and death. As he enters the kitchen of the hotel where he is staying, a young girl screams, "supposing [him] to be a spirit"; but her screams are drowned out by David's own screams, albeit screams muffled by fear and dread and thus finding their proper voice in the deafening sounds of the wind and ocean.

For one who has anticipated his own death as profoundly as David does in this chapter, it becomes a tranquilizing experience to write of the deaths of others, even of those deeply loved, in so far as it restores once again a narrative that contains order and coherence. Images without intelligibility become transformed into a history in which the boundaries between the dream and the actual, between life and death, are given definition and projected outside of oneself. Thus it is that the ostensible conclusion to this chapter—the description of the deaths of Ham and Steerforth—really begins and ends in less than two pages. A strange serenity seems to pervade the chapter's concluding paragraph: "And on that part of it [the shore] where she and I had looked for shells, two children— on that part of it where some lighter fragments of the old boat, blown down last night, had been scattered by the wind—among the ruins of the home he had wronged—I saw him lying with his head upon his arm, as I had often seen him lie at school." The images themselves are, of course, not necessarily consoling, suggesting, as they do, images of childhood and youth broken and scattered like the old ship-home. Yet, unlike the earlier images of the chapter, these are controlled and nonthreatening. They suggest a death or dissolution that can be both comprehended and confronted; memory can accommodate them and impose upon them a sad but quiet serenity, one that encloses the narrator and those who have died within a vision in which the narrator can silence that terror of separation and discontinuity that lies behind much of the power and beauty of the chapter.

*So was it with me then, and so will be*
*With Poets ever. Mighty is the charm*
*Of those abstractions to a mind beset*
*With images, and haunted by itself.*
WORDSWORTH, *The Prelude*

After the "Tempest" chapter where does the nineteenth-century novel, and *David Copperfield* in particular, go? In what ways can it cope with a knowledge found in the realms of darkness and dreams, and how can it translate that knowledge into the language and structure of the novel? Except for isolated scenes and episodes, the outside world of *David Copperfield* does not seem large enough to accommodate the soul of the mature narrator or to allow it full expression. The soul is contained within the circle of its own knowledge, a knowledge that is destined to be falsified or forgotten once the hero enters into the world of social convention and orthodox values, however admirable they might be. In order to complete his own Memorial, and to return once again to those spaces from which he has departed when he began his imaginative "solitary pilgrimage," he must once again confront those images, but he must also finally deny or forget them. There is not, in spite of a courageous search for one, a permanent correspondence or identity between the center of the circle (the narrator's memory and imagination) and its periphery, that social landscape he traverses. The hero must either move away from himself by fleeing into that periphery and an ultimately inadequate consolation (evidenced by his need to take flight once again) or by assimilating the world into his own private vision, by forcing the ideal upon the real and by projecting himself as the hero of an extremely precarious vision.

This vision is precarious because it is threatened by time. Youth in *David Copperfield* can triumph over time only by means of an early death, by a violent crashing-out from the oncoming world which those left behind still must face. The hero as youth, whether the inarticulated heroism of a Ham or the demon-ridden heroism of a Steerforth, can retain his heroism only by moving outside of time, by becoming the image that David retains of Steerforth "fast asleep, lying, easily, with his hand upon his arm, as I had often seen him lie at school." To remain behind, on the other hand, is to face one's own future coming toward one, a future whose possibilites are conjured up by the image of the "poor lunatic gentleman" in David's old room. Fairly late in the novel, David reflects upon impressions that "slumbered, and half awoke, and slept again, in the innermost recesses of my mind," and here Dickens posits a type of heroism which he will explore more fully in *Great Expectations*. In this construction, the hero possesses what Lukács has described as "virile maturity," the capacity to realize both that the ideal and the real can never coincide, and that he must still continue to search for precisely such a coincidence.

> What I missed, I still regarded—I always regarded—as something that had been a dream of my youthful fancy; that was incapable of realisation; that I was now discovering to be so, with some natural pain, as all men did. But that it would have been better for me if my wife could have helped me more, and shared the many thoughts in which I had no partner; and that this might have been; I knew.
>
> Because these two irreconcilable conclusions; the one, that what I felt was general and unavoidable; the other, that it was particular to me, and might have been different; I balanced curiously, with no distinct sense of their opposition to each other. When I thought of the airy dreams of youth that are incapable of realisation, I thought of the better state preceding manhood that I had outgrown. And then the contented days with Agnes, in the dear old house, arose before me, like spectres of the dead, that might have some renewal in another world, but never more could be reanimated here.

The "irreconcilable conclusions" within this passage extend beyond a solitary clash between the general and the particular; what we see here is a clash between the ideal and the real, of that which should be with that which is. As David realizes, what he perceives are equal but opposing truths incapable of resolution or synthesis. This passage also contains evidence of a tension arising from a mind at odds with the direction of its own movement, one engaged in the process of self-revelation while also attempting to conceal or mitigate the implications of the revelation. In this case David's recognition of these mutually exclusive and irreconcilable positions is muted, as it were, by a mode of perception that helps to muffle or alleviate the pain he feels. He moves toward a mystified past and a mystified future—toward the past's "better state preceding manhood" and the future's promise of a repetition of the mystified past, "of the contented days with Agnes in the dear old house . . . that might have some renewal in another world, but never more could be reanimated here." The directions of this passage suggest the real and enduring threat that time poses to the man who journeys forth in order to redeem it. This threat is disarmed, however, by the movement toward a mission that is almost static, one that conceives of a reality beyond time and also beyond humanity. Because the above passage is both honest and courageous, it elicits our admiration, but at the same time it also elicits sadness, for, by the end of the novel, the tensions evident in it have disappeared, absorbed within a vision that conceals the natural pain David shares with all men.

If *David Copperfield* fails to find a world that can adequately reflect its hero's depths, Dickens's struggle to envision such a world makes his novel a magnificent work, one whose power is evidenced in that at times faltering, at times prophetic, structure into which his vision unfolds. The movement of the novel is at odds with itself: while the journey undertaken is essentially an imaginative one, one that moves with greatest energy when the region being traversed is that of a man beset and haunted by images that compel him on his journey, it is within the public order and its social structures that the novel must attempt to define and reveal David's interior. *David Copperfield* suggests only partial awareness of the widening chasm that developed in nineteenth-century fiction between the public and private vision; after all, a good part of the novel is concerned with what David should do and what he wants to do. At the same time, the tensions within it that arise from his inability to find self-definition within the public modes of fulfillment (the only appropriate livelihood for him is that of the artist, for it is private and yet makes possible public communication and rewards) tend to thrust the narrator further into himself. The circus and Coketown have not yet been cast asunder; one can still, with some effort, find it possible for work and play, prudence and spontaneity, to exist side by side. Wemmick is certainly anticipated by Traddles, but Walworth can still reside, though surreptitiously, for Traddles within the city limits.

The demonic or irrational forces that are in part responsible for the confusion of Mr. Dick and David also help one to withstand or subvert that world of reason and domination understood so well by Miss Mowcher. Traddles acknowledges, through the skeletons he is forever drawing, those demons that accompany him and keep his hair unruly. When Traddles enters public life, he maintains his concealed garden of Eros, a hidden and private enclosure whose "domestic arrangements are, to say the truth, quite unprofessional." Within this enclosure Traddles, his wife, and her sisters engage in kissing, romping, and playing at "Puss in the Corner." They stand out in "that withered Gray's Inn" as much as if "the Sultan's famous family had been admitted on the roll of attorneys, and had brought the talking bird, the singing tree, and the golden water into Gray's Inn Hall." Admittedly, Eros has been transformed in this scene into the cherubic Cupid that adorned so many Victorian valentines, yet the implications of the scene—the contrast established between work and play, between sexuality and the "withered Gray's Inn"—verify Steven Marcus's observations of how Dickens and other great nineteenth-century artists humanized and amplified those metaphors that are more vividly and less complexly seen in Victorian pornography.

The history of Traddles is further evidence of the difficulty Dickens encountered in translating David's interior drama and conflict into action and adventure. Death, exile, emigration, or a perpetually maintained duality and deception (as in Traddles's case) more in the cause of survival than subversion seem frequently to be the avenues whereby the novel's perception is converted into action. In fact, among the major characters of the novel only Mr. Peggotty can express and fulfull himself through action. Led through suffering and wandering on a journey that embodies his own mythic capacities, Mr. Peggotty transcends and transforms the world through which he travels. Like the classic heroes whose pattern he repeats, he is preceded by his own legend during a journey that sanctifies and transfigures the world: as David writes, "everything seemed, to my imagination, to be hushed in reverence for him, as he resumed his solitary journey through the snow." Peggotty's search transcends the limits of an individual mission and almost assumes the stature of a religious pilgrimage.

> "By little and little, when I come to a new village or that, among the poor people, I found they know'd about me. They would set me down at their cottage doors, and give me whatnot fur to eat and drink, and show me wheer to sleep; and many a woman, Mas'r Davy, as had a daughter of about Em'ly's age, I've found a-waiting for me at Our Saviour's Cross, outside the village, fur to do me sim'lar kindnesses. Some has had daughters

> as was dead. And God only knows how good them mothers was to me! . . ."
>
> "They would often put their children—partic'lar their little girls," said Mr. Peggotty, "upon my knee; and many a time you might have seen me sitting at their doors, when night was coming on, a'most as if they'd been my Darling's children. Oh, my Darling!"

These passages, however, also reveal how close Dickens came to losing control over the figure of Peggotty, finding it difficult, undoubtedly, to translate an almost perfect goodness into dialogue and action. This same precariousness also suggests the hold this figure had on Dickens's imagination: throughout the novel Peggotty's fulfillment, and even his suffering, stands out against the fulfillment, and the suffering, of the novel's hero.

There are indications toward the later part of the novel that Dickens is trying to depict within the narrative a correspondence between recognition and action on David's part, but it is finally a correspondence forced upon the novel. In the final denouement of Uriah Heep, for example, an action that results from the combined efforts of Traddles and Micawber, Dickens brings David into the scene and gives him an active participation far in excess of his actual role by having Uriah direct his anger against David instead of against the real agents of his fall: " 'Why, there's Copperfield, mother,' he angrily retorted, pointing his lean finger at me, against whom all his animosity was levelled, as the prime mover in the discovery; and I did not undeceive him; 'there's Copperfield, would have given you a hundred pounds to say less than you've blurted out!' " Throughout the scene David is a passive, indeed bewildered, spectator, not knowing even when arriving at Micawber's office what was going to happen or what had been done; yet in trying to bring David actively into it (even at the cost of duplicity on David's part) and to pit him against his old adversary, Dickens gives him a role of active participation with which his hero is uncomfortable. In fact, in the final exchange between the two, Uriah seems almost to emerge the victor, penetrating in his remarks to the canker of hypocrisy within the body politic that Dickens would examine again: " 'They used to teach me at school (the same where I picked up so much umbleness), from nine o'clock to eleven, that labour was a curse; and from eleven o'clock to one, that it was a blessing and a cheerfulness, and a dignity, and I don't know what all, eh? Won't umbleness go down? I shouldn't have got round my gentleman partner without it, I think.' " This speech is not answered by David: its truth does not permit refutation; it can only be ignored.

In chapter 57 ("Absence") Dickens continues to seek for a language and a metaphor capable of defining and amplifying David's pilgrimage. However, neither the language nor the metaphor suffices, for they are borrowed from a tradition whose sources of strength Dickens can no longer draw upon. David's journey into Switzerland and into the isolation which finally leads to a renewed integration with mankind is in one respect absolutely correct as metaphor. At the same time, however, it finally belies those truths that it brings forth. The chapter's early descriptions capture with great power that psychic landscape into which David has been cast, a landscape corresponding to the hero's own moods and reflections: "It was a long and gloomy night that gathered on me, haunted by the ghosts of many hopes, of many dear remembrances, many errors, many unavailing sorrows and regrets." Traveling through "a ruined blank and waste, lying wide around me, unbroken, to the dark horizon," David approaches, albeit unwittingly and unwillingly, an intimation of man's place in this world, one that will be further defined in Dickens's later novels, such as *Great Expectations* and *Our Mutual Friend*. In this chapter, as in the "Tempest" chapter, we see the hero confronting himself without illusion: "I roamed from place to place, carrying my burden with me everywhere. I felt its whole weight now; and I drooped beneath it, and I said in my heart that it could never be lightened."

But the unbroken horizon and the unsheltered spaces are too threatening; their vastness and lack of definition are too frightening. The hero is in danger of exploding, of disappearing into a world unmarked by those literary and social demarcations established by his predecessors. When Dickens confronts the deepest (and, I think, the truest) impulses of his imagination, he discovers in them that terror of discontinuity and separation which Geoffrey Hartmann finds in Wordsworth. The images from *David Copperfield* that remain with us—the graveyard, the lunatic gentleman, the entire "Tempest" episode—are those that give expression, or at least recognition, to such impulses. It is fitting that it is in *Copperfield,* the most Wordsworthian of Dickens's novels, that we see the hero seeking an affirmation of continuity in Nature; it finally provides him, however, with even less solace than it provided his imaginative predecessor. Like the poet, David is unsuccessful in discovering in Nature a reprieve from the primacy of his own imagination. In the novel the natural world is devoid of rectifying powers or transcendental immanence: in it, Nature stands in a distant relationship to man: "I had found sublimity and wonder in the dread heights and precipices [of the Alps], in the roaring torrents, and the wastes of ice and snow; but as yet, I had found nothing else." Even this "sublimity and wonder" seems a feeble descriptive phrase, more like emotions David should have felt than emotions verified by the scene. Thus David's description of Nature several paragraphs later is unexpected and unwarranted, the sudden intrusion (and equally sudden disappearance) of Nature as an instrumentality within a work from which it has been conspicuously absent: "All at once, in this serenity, great Nature spoke to me; and soothed me to lay my weary head upon the grass, and weep as I had not wept yet, since Dora died! . . . I resorted humbly whither Agnes had commended me; I sought out Nature, never sought in vain; and I admitted to my breast the human interest I had lately shrunk from."

It is difficult to believe in the above passages; Dickens has not earned the right to draw so heavily upon such a metaphor, and the fact that he would do so suggests the intensity of his search for a language or a metaphor that could viably accommodate and define his hero. Dickens could have waged such a struggle for only so long before sensing that there was no metaphor capable of adequately resolving the dissonances within his hero; in one respect the "Absence" chapter signals David's escape from the burdens of selfhood. It initiates his reintegration with mankind and leads rather quickly to his marriage with Agnes. The tensions within the novel seem to disappear and David moves toward a world quite different from the one he had known before. He moves out of one tormented by anxieties and into one in which the recalcitrant self and the outer world are harmoniously wedded—until, that is, the self emerges again to pursue the forever elusive image of complete reconciliation.

The form of the romance emerges victorious and absorbs into itself that Romantic artist whose quest must remain internal, waging within himself a battle whose outcome will determine the death or survival of the imagination. Once *David Copperfield* assumes its final form, it fulfills both its own destiny and its own death. The hero is absorbed into a social vision of fulfillment as well as into his own silence. The tensions between the ideal and the real have apparently disappeared, and we are presented with an artistic vision (enclosed within the metaphor of domesticity) of a world within which man is no longer alienated. Yet David still lives within that world he has previously presented to us. Thus, in order for the novel's final vision to be realized, he must become increasingly more alienated from that deeper voice and vision he has heard and seen. When David enters those spaces where "everything was as it used to be, in the happy time," where Agnes has been busy "in keeping everything as it used to be when we were children," we witness the silencing of a profound imagination.

Once the tensions within the novel disappear, it comes fairly rapidly to its conclusion, with a final vision whose loss of complexity is seen in the humorous, but easy, transition into comparatively orthodox social and moral satire (Heep and Littimer in prison, and the dialogue between David and Mr. Chillip about the Murdstones). Neither is really required, but they do suggest Dickens's attempt, partly successful, to give renewed vitality to a work he perhaps sensed was moving too rapidly toward closure. But Dickens is too honest and perceptive an artist to bury the images of his novel for long; thus we see them reappear, transformed but identifiable, in his following novels: in the winds that travel from David to *Bleak House* (there to trouble and perplex Mr. Jarndyce), in the widening chasm seen between public and private myths of fulfillment in the dual narrative structure of *Bleak House* and in the circus and Coketown of *Hard Times*, in the progressively increasing distance between the interior and the exterior that we find in *Little Dorrit* and *Great Expectations*.

But if *David Copperfield* promises its hero a gratification that will become more tenuous or suspect in Dickens's later novels, we see even here what is perhaps Dickens's final uneasiness about the novel's conclusion (his own admission, although obliquely presented) that the spaces he has created may not be able to fulfill all that they promise. The passages I have in mind occur at the end of the novel and concern the changed Julia Mills.

> But Julia keeps no diary in these days; never sings Affection's Dirge; eternally quarrels with the old Scotch Croesus, who is a sort of yellow bear with a tanned hide. Julia is steeped in money to the throat, and talks and thinks of nothing else. I liked her better in the Desert of Sahara. Or perhaps this *is* the Desert of Sahara. For, though Julia has a stately house, and mighty company, and sumptuous dinners every day, I see no green growth near her; nothing that can ever come to fruit or flower. . . . When society is the name for such hollow gentlemen and ladies, Julia, and when its breeding is professed indifference to everything that can advance or can retard mankind, I think we must have lost ourselves in the same Desert of Sahara, and had better find the way out.

The crucial questions in this passage—the location and precise configuration of the Desert of Sahara—remain only ambiguously answered. When we reflect on the passage, we can see the antithesis established—between the Desert on the one hand and the green and fecund garden on the other—is precarious and problematic. We are to read it, most certainly, as the observation of a man who himself lives within the "green growth," participating in a world wherein things do indeed "come to fruit or flower."

There is no self-irony intended, nor are we justified in regarding the passage in such a light, but we should be aware of the inherent fragility of the landscape out of which the hero makes his judgments: if the hero has come full circle to the point from which he began his narrative, in so doing he has woven about him a sphere that is vulnerable to destruction. Julia Mills's silence echoes the silence both of Mr. Dick and the silence that will soon envelop David. Each is absorbed into a world that will dispel the images of which he or she wrote and spoke. Their voices, however, die quietly and painlessly; they can still speak, if only of things that conceal the very loss they have incurred. And if for now the Desert of Sahara is confined to that part of society that is dead and deadening, it cannot be held off for long by the warmth and love of the immediate world-garden that surrounds David. It will eventually encroach on this gentle fortress until the final images of the novel are turned inside out and the garden located on the perimeters of civilization. When the Desert has achieved ultimate success, it transforms the landscape into one which death has triumphed over life. Madness becomes the image of reason having satiated its own appetite, and David's virtues of earnestness, industry, and thrift become the signposts of a world controlled and ravaged by Smallweeds and Bounderbys. But while there are indications of latent doubt at the end of *David Copperfield,* they are presented in such a way that the conclusion is not seriously disturbed or violated. These doubts are, however, destined to reappear and demand a new confrontation in the novels that follow.

At the end of *David Copperfield,* the narrator's final voice seems to bespeak an alienation from the self that he has sought, found, and then lost. The hero seeks protection within an enclosure that finds its final image in the green and fruitful garden. But this garden has been created by the alienation of the hero and its existence depends on the perpetuity of certain assumptions, which, while they may appear solid and substantial in the light of day, are threatened by those images of the dark, images that tell of a history that does lie, of a past that does not contain its dead, and of a future that promises only the terror (and the joy) of becoming what one is.

It is appropriate, finally, that *David Copperfield* is a novel about a novelist writing a novel while denying that he is writing a novel at all. For it is a novel about the novel, one that contains its genre's history and also prefigures its genre's future. It is a novel that speaks of alienation while attesting to its own alienation. On the one hand it seeks solace and protection within the structures of its form, while on the other hand it expresses the limits and weakness of the form and engages in rebellion against them.

Struggling with a tradition that provides it with an ambivalent comfort, it must borrow the vocabulary and structures of that tradition in order to wage battle against it. Dickens gazes deeply into the inner regions of the self and hears from within image-haunted winds, but what he sees and hears sends him back toward the protection of definition and form. There he must deny, or attempt to deny, those demonic voices that sing of freedom and its terrors. The world of *David Copperfield* is richly inhabited by those heroes of whom the young and lonely David has read: "Roderick Random, Peregrine Pickle, Humphrey Clinker, Tom Jones, the Vicar of Wakefield, Don Quixote, Gil Blas, and Robinson Crusoe, . . . they, and the Arabian Nights, and the Tales of the Genii." But these heroes and the worlds they move in are not David's, even though they posit values and beliefs that will endure. For the landscape of *David Copperfield* is one that explores regions previously unexplored in English fiction. The rich tradition of the novel that Dickens drew upon was able to help him explore the landscape and could provide him with support and comfort, but it was capable of only partially demarcating the world through which his hero traverses. And even though we do see a movement back into the tradition, the realm into which David journeys beckons forth to those novels that are yet to come, just as surely as David himself is beckoned forth by his image-ridden memory.

# *David Copperfield:* The Trial of Realism

*John P. McGowan*

In March 1850, when *David Copperfield* was still eight installments from completion, the first issue of *Household Words* appeared. In "A Preliminary Word" to his new magazine, Dickens pledges to "tenderly cherish that light of Fancy which is inherent in the human breast" and to "show to all, that in all familiar things, even in those which are repellant on the surface, there is Romance enough, if we will find it out." It would be impossible to prove that this championing of fancy is the result of the experience of writing *David Copperfield,* but the timing of the defense is suggestive. In this essay I will discuss the nature of *David Copperfield*'s realism and, subsequently, the problems the attempt to write a realistic novel presented to Dickens. My general contention is that the failure of this novel's realism gave Dickens a new appreciation of fancy's claims, and led to the aesthetic of fancy articulated by Dickens for the first time in "A Preliminary Word" and defended by him throughout the rest of his career, most notably in *Hard Times*.

In a recently published book, Robert Newsom, starting from the reiteration in the preface to *Bleak House* of "A Preliminary Word" 's promise to reveal the romance in familiar things, discusses that novel's "play . . . between the empirical and the fictional" (*Dickens on the Romantic Side of Familiar Things:* Bleak House *and the Novel Tradition*). While touching on issues I discuss here, Newsom's view is much more dialectical, focusing on the relation of fiction to the real, whereas I wish to discuss the existence

From *Nineteenth-Century Fiction* 34, no. 1 (June 1979). 

of realism and fancy side by side in a novel in which they both exist even though they contradict one another. The difference between our arguments is related, at least in part, to Newsom's discussing a novel written after Dickens's explicit statement of the aesthetic of fancy and my discussing a novel written before that statement.

The distinction between realism and fancy with which I shall begin is a simple one. Realism is that literary mode which stresses language's ability to repeat or represent accurately in words the world of things, whereas fancy focuses on the difference between the world of objects and a linguistic world, thus emphasizing what imagination adds when it undertakes to describe the world "out there." In *Adam Bede,* George Eliot states the realist's desire simply to describe the world as it is. She recognizes that the novelist might use fancy to "refashion life and character entirely after [her] own liking," but informs the reader that she will "avoid any such arbitrary picture." Jacques Derrida, among contemporary theorists of language, has discussed most fully what the user of language adds when he describes the world in words, and my discussion will depend on issues Derrida has made familiar: representation, repetition, and the difference between words and things. *David Copperfield* presents the distinction between realism and fancy as follows:

> When my thoughts go back now, to that slow agony of my youth, I wonder how much of the histories I invented for such people hangs like a mist of fancy over well-remembered facts! When I tread the old ground, I do not wonder that I seem to see and pity, going on before me, an innocent romantic boy, making his imaginative world out of such strange experiences and sordid things.

"Fancy" is confronted with "fact" here, just as it will be in *Hard Times,* but in this case the narrator's sympathy is with fact. Fancy is all right for the child, especially if he needs to retreat from a world of "sordid things" which he cannot change. But for an adult, for a narrator who wishes to present the facts about his life clearly and accurately, fancy only threatens the integrity of his narrative. David must sift through his memories, separating fact from fancy. The only crime which David ever admits is that he was "romantic"; at the end of his narrative, he will attribute the troubles of his adult life to following the dictates of a childish, "heedless fancy." David's progress leads him from a childhood "romanticism" toward a staunch reliance on and, at times, stoical acceptance of "the reality principle," a movement thematized as the maturation of an "undisciplined heart." Or, at least, that is the way David likes to present his progress. As we shall see, fancy has more to do with David's story than he, as a realistic narrator, is prepared to admit.

A realistic narrative must establish what is indisputably "real." In *David Copperfield* this privileged position is accorded to immediate perceptual experience, primarily the visual and the aural. The second chapter of the novel, entitled "I Observe," establishes the primacy of the visual. The chapter begins: "The first objects that assume a distinct presence before me, as I look far back, into the blank of my infancy, are my mother . . . and Peggotty." Seeing things is the way in which they are established as "objects," as separate from the perceiving self, yet present to that self, as immediately real as it is.

Memory is another kind of seeing, as the phrase "look far back" in the passage just quoted indicates. If memory's "seeing" is not merely metaphorical, but as accurate as the original seeing, then the narrative as a "written memory" will simply record the discoveries of that looking back. And David takes pains to characterize himself as an exceptionally observant person throughout his life. "I looked at nothing, that I know of, but I saw everything, even to the prospect of a church upon his china inkstand, as I sat down—and this, too, was a faculty confirmed in me in the old Micawber times."

The primary reality of the visual is asserted by contrasting it to the fanciful in a passage which gathers together several of the novel's most central concerns.

> One Sunday night my mother reads to Peggotty and me in there [the room in which his father's funeral was held], how Lazarus was raised up from the dead. And I am so frightened that they are afterwards obliged to take me out of bed, and show me the quiet churchyard out of the bedroom window, with the dead all lying in their graves at rest, below the solemn moon.
>
> There is nothing half so green that I know anywhere, as the grass of that churchyard; nothing half so shady as its trees; nothing half so quiet as its tombstones. The sheep are feeding there, when I kneel up, early in the morning, in my little bed in a closet within my mother's room, to look out at it; and I see the red light shining on the sun-dial, and think within myself, "Is the sun-dial glad, I wonder, that it can tell the time again?"

The visual fact of the quiet churchyard is presented to the child to quell the fanciful fears awakened by the story. The clarity of daytime vision is contrasted to the fancies of nighttime, romantic visions developed in the dark when nothing real can be seen. The return of the sun at dawn means the return of the outside world to the child—and this daytime world of consciousness and visual perception is the world of time. Only with the sunrise does time begin, as the question to the sundial indicates. David clearly associates consciousness with the ability to see things. "I felt so sleepy, that I knew if I lost sight of anything, for a moment, I was gone." Consciousness is that condition in which we remain aware of the outer world, and the most important awareness is visual.

Yet, interestingly enough, the reality which so completely dominates David's childhood vision, the landscape which seems more green, more shady, more quiet than anything else, is the churchyard, with its reminders of death, particularly the gravestone which marks the father's resting place. David is quieted down by being assured that the dead remain dead, that the story of Lazarus is not real. In a world of objects present to his sight, the child is fascinated by the object—a tombstone—which is a memorial to an absent object. This passage already suggests the limits of a reliance on a purely visual apprehension of reality. A historical world has a depth which cannot be comprehended by the purely visual; things which are absent, which cannot be seen now, have a bearing on the significance of that which is seen in the present moment. But, at this early stage in the narrative, explicit awareness of this complication is avoided, while David celebrates, as Wordsworth was wont to do, the union of the child with his immediate surroundings.

Aural perceptions do not receive as much attention as visual ones, but they are also classed among immediate perceptions of the real, establishing contact between the self and the outside world. Hearing is most important when sight is deprived; in normal cases, hearing is simply linked with seeing, since we hear as well as see the person speaking in front of us. However, when locked into his room after biting Murdstone, David has to rely entirely on hearing to gain information of the outside world. "I listened to all the incidents of the house that made themselves audible to me; the ringing of bells, the opening and shutting of doors, the murmuring of voices, the footsteps on the stairs; to any laughing, whistling, or singing, outside, which seemed more dismal than anything else to me in my solitude and disgrace." Hearing, like seeing, involves a perception of the present moment; a nearby sound is heard in the moment in which it is made. But since seeing is primary, when we cannot see what is making a sound we need to interpret the noise in order to understand who or what caused it. Thus aural perception, when unaccompanied by the presence of the causal agent to sight, already implies a distance from the external world, albeit a spatial, not a temporal, distance. The primacy of sight rests on its exclusion of all such distance, its immediate union of self and world.

The clarity of daytime vision is often contrasted to the confusion of dreams, but this is not the case in David's narrative. Several chapters in the first half of the novel end with his falling asleep, and with a short account of his dreams. (Chapters 6, 7, 8, 14, 19, 24, and 25 all mention David's dreams on the last page of each chapter.) The last page of chapter 7 is fairly typical: "I had many a broken sleep inside the Yarmouth mail, and many an incoherent dream of all these things. But when I awoke at intervals, the ground outside the window was not the playground of Salem House, and the sound in my ears was not the sound of Mr. Creakle giving it to Traddles, but was the sound of the coachman touching up the horses." The dreams in the novel break down into isolated perceptions, in this case both visual and aural, having no plot, and usually being simple repetitions of the images of the day just past. Focusing on the imagistic content of dreams assures their "incoherence" in terms of narrative structure. This places dreams in an odd position, epistemologically, in the novel. Dreams are "realistic" insofar as they present aural and visual images, and as such, the dreams in the narrative are usually easily recognizable as representations of David's experiences. However, dreams are nonrealistic, "fanciful," insofar as these images float free of context, notably narrative context.

This odd position of dreams is tied to the narrative's commitment to the factual as opposed to the fanciful quality of memory; it is important to David as narrator that the memories presented in the narrative be established as accurate. The images of memory are, in several ways, obviously akin to those of dreams, so the narrative takes pains to establish the perceptual accuracy of both. The difference between memory and dream is that memory can construct a coherent narrative account by which its images are organized temporally.

Dream images and memory are most obviously alike in the way they differ from the images of sense perception. Hume has offered the traditional distinction between the two types of images by calling those of dream and memory "ideas" and those of sense perception "impressions." Hume's insistence that impressions are always more "lively" than ideas is questionable, since a vivid dream or memory is often more pronounced than a weak sensory perception. David offers his own counter example to Hume, when he writes of Traddles: "His honest face . . . impresses me more in the remembrance than it did in the reality." This ability of memory to see details clearly, perhaps even more clearly than at the moment of original perception, is crucial to the narrative's insistence on its accuracy.

"Ideas" (in Hume's sense) are suspect because they do not rely on the object's presence, whereas an "impression" is generated by an object present to the perceiver. The problem with second-order images, those "ideas" formed in the object's absence, is that their faithfulness to the thing represented is not immediately verifiable; these ideas might be fanciful. In *David Copperfield*, that fancy alters or remakes the world in imagination is assumed, but the narrative tries to keep memory, and even dream images, out of fancy's camp. Of course, some dream distortion is admitted, but since dream images are similar to those of memory, the clarity of dreams is stressed in order to help establish the reliability of memory.

Thus, when David comes to narrate "an event in my life, so indelible, so awful" that his whole narrative has been directed toward it, he combines dream and memory to assert the faithfulness of his narration to the original:

> For years after it occurred, I dreamed of it often. I have started up so vividly impressed by it, that its fury has yet seemed raging in my quiet room, in the still night. I dream of it sometimes, though at lengthened and uncertain intervals, to this hour. I have an association between it and a stormy wind, or the lightest mention of a sea-shore, as strong as any of which my mind is conscious. As plainly as I behold what happened, I will try to write it down. I do not recall it, but see it done; for it happens again before me.

Determined to validate the accuracy of his narrative, David appeals to the perceptual situation in which the object is present to the viewer. Memory can "see" so clearly that David can insist that the original event is not temporally distant, not permanently lost in the past; it exists in the present and, because present, is seen. "I do not recall it, but see it done; for it happens again before me." In this instance, there is no temporal absence; the event has been present in dream and memory to David throughout the years since it took place.

This is the "realism" for which David's narrative strives: a point where the images of memory are overwhelmed by the lost object's return to presence, to immediate perception. By locating the real in immediate sensory perception, David can only assert the "reality" of his memory when it yields to such immediacy. Ideally, the images of memory, and the words David uses to convey those images, are transparent, opening toward an apprehension of the event which was their genesis—an apprehension that is the same as having actually witnessed the event.

"Realism" is the attempt to guarantee that all representations are exact copies of the original; that words serve as simple, faithful, and transparent denominations of things; that meaning is something which exists separate of words and which is made manifest by words. Realism is essentially hostile to time; its most fundamental desire is to regain the past, to repeat that past exactly in the present, denying that anything is lost irrevocably. This demand for the lost object's return to presence is the repudiation of all representations, all substitutes, in favor of the thing itself. It is the impossibility of this desire, recognized dimly, as we shall see, in David's narrative, even while he strives to fulfill it, which leads to Dickens's absolute abandonment of realism in the celebration of "Fancy" in the 1850s.

Realism's hostility to time, its attempt to deny death, is one reason Dickens eventually abandons it; another is its hostility to words. The realist aspires to silence, the mute apprehension of actual things. David evidences some of the realist's mistrust of words, of their tendency to get between the perceiver and that which is to be perceived. In search of a transparent style, David often expresses his belief that metaphorical and rhetorical flourishes crowd out the real. A simple instance occurs in one of his attempts to be "serious" with Dora. He tells her: "We infect everyone about us" and then comments on this way of stating his "meaning." "I might have gone on in this figurative manner, if Dora's face had not admonished me that she was wondering with all her might whether I was going to propose any new kind of vaccination, or other medical remedy, for this unwholesome state of ours. Therefore I checked myself, and made my meaning plainer." Figurative language is directly contrasted with making one's meaning "plain," and David, as usual when he is explicit about the type of language he prefers, chooses the latter. (Of course, his narration as a whole is full of metaphors, just as it has a "style," but these are not explicitly acknowledged).

David's "transparent style" is implicitly compared with Micawber's use of language throughout the novel. Style as tyranny, as the imposition of one's particular point of view on another, is represented by Micawber—and is why that comic figure is as threatening a father figure as Murdstone. Micawber's extravagance, both financial and linguistic, is dangerous in its subjection of other people. Traddles "loans his name" to Micawber; this ominous phrase combines the linguistic and the financial, placing Traddles within the world Micawber has constituted for himself to serve his own purposes. David must avoid Traddles's mistake, must hold on to his own name, and forge a style of his own. The Micawbers belong to the warehouse world, a world to which David is introduced by Murdstone, and from which he must escape.

Both Murdstone and Micawber try to impose a certain world upon the child, a world most easily identified by its language; Murdstone's puritanical vocabulary is as distinctive as Micawber's florid style. David must reject both as inadequate; the process of his maturation is, in part, the process of developing his own style. However, that style is never recognized as one. Rather, the narrative acts as if its own style were transparent, with no tinge of self. The Murdstone and Micawber languages are idiosyncratic and hence objectionable. Their styles are personal and imply a refusal to participate in the human community, but David, using "ordinary" language, establishes a "pure" communication with others, one which simply states what has happened. (This negative description of Micawber emphasizes his similarity to Pecksniff, but since *David Copperfield,* as we shall see, both recognizes, albeit dimly, and makes use of Micawber-type language, Micawber is treated more kindly [banished to triumph in Australia rather than caned] than the earlier extravagant talker.)

The most complete denunciation of words and their use to obscure meaning, to prevent a clear apprehension of the real, comes in a discussion of Micawber's language. This passage is worthy of the third book of Locke's *Essay Concerning Human Understanding* in its plea for a plain style in which words are fitted to things.

> Mr. Micawber had a relish in this formal piling up of words, which, however ludicrously displayed in his case, was, I must say, not at all peculiar to him. I have observed it, in the course of my life, in numbers of men. It seems to me to be a general rule. . . . We talk about the tyranny of words, but we like to tyrannise over them too; we are fond of having a large superfluous establishment of words to wait upon us on great occasions; we think it looks important, and sounds well. As we are not particular about the meaning of our liveries on state occasions, if they be but fine and numerous enough, so the meaning or necessity of our words is a secondary consideration, if there be but a great parade of them. And as individuals get into trouble by making too great a show of liveries, or as slaves when they are too numerous rise against their masters, so I think I could mention a nation that has got into many great difficulties, and will get into many greater, from maintaining too large a retinue of words.

A remarkable passage, in which we find a writer complaining that we have "too large a retinue of words," many of which are superfluous. Our extravagance with words, which leads to a disregard of "meaning," is declared to be a "general rule," but the form of David's critique makes it clear that he feels he avoids the worst abuses. Micawber's use of language, marvelous as it is, is finally seen as abusive, and he is banished to Australia.

Yet this hostility to words is not consistently maintained throughout the narrative, and in considering David's attitudes toward language we shall discover the implicit critique of realism found in this novel which struggles to be realistic. Even Micawber will be found to have a legitimate place in those instances when the novel relies on, rather than bemoans, the difference between words and things.

The first indication of this difference is the child's fascination with the physical properties of words. David's reliance on sensory perception insures that words, as peculiar sensory experiences, will interest him. Spoken words can be heard, but not seen; written words can be seen, but not heard. David experiences the material existence of the spoken word when trying to communicate with Peggotty through the keyhole after he has been locked in his room for biting Murdstone. "I was obliged to get her to repeat it, for she spoke it the first time quite down my throat, in consequence of my having forgotten to take my mouth away from the keyhole and put my ear there; and though her words tickled me a good deal, I didn't hear them." This experience suggests that when the material qualitites of words attract our attention, we begin to lose our sense of what the words mean. The word's existence in itself as a material thing conflicts with its function as a sign of something else.

David is also fascinated by the appearance of the written word. "To this day, when I look upon the fat black letters in the primer, the puzzling novelty of their shapes, and the easy good-nature of O and Q and S, seem to present themselves again before me as they used to do." Written letters "present themselves" to the viewer as objects in their own right, as physical things which have form and color. The struggles to learn shorthand repeat this preoccupation with the physical shapes of signs, as well as suggesting that when the signs' novelty wears off, we become less aware of their physical presence and more willing to see them only in terms of what they are meant to represent. "The most despotic characters I have ever known; who insisted, for instance, that a thing like the beginning of a cobweb, meant expectation, and that a pen-and-ink sky-rocket stood for disadvantageous." Of course, if the fact that the sign looks like a sky-rocket is emphasized, its standing for disadvantageous will seem absurd. These "arbitrary characters" become "despotic" at the moment when David looks at them as if they were not arbitrary, as if their physical appearance were a clue to their conventional meaning as signs.

When handwriting is involved, however, physical appearances are not so arbitrary. How a person writes is as important an indication of his or her character as what he or she writes. David is able to guess accurately the characters of Steerforth and Traddles simply by examining their carved signatures on an old door at Salem House. Peggotty's letters are incomprehensible in all the ordinary senses of the word, but their physical appearance is "more expressive . . . than the best composition." Jack Maldon and Mr. Dick are implicitly contrasted within a few pages of each other in terms of their writing skills, with Maldon's "numerous mistakes" placed alongside Mr. Dick's "extraordinary neatness." When Traddles's Sophy suppresses all her femininity to write "masculine" legal script, it serves as final proof of her self-denying character. A person's handwriting becomes a kind of "objective correlative," an outward manifestation of his personality. This same connection does not apply to the printed word, since its appearance is completely arbitrary and impersonal. The printed word's physical appearance will only distract us from its sense.

David's naive perceptual experience of letters and words as physical objects, while conforming to his tendency to privilege sensory perception, involves the recognition of the word's essential difference from the thing. And this essential difference must undermine literary realism. There can be no exact repetition; a repetition in words or in memory is a repetition by representative, a repetition with a difference. David's narrative hedges on this point; it both accepts and denies that repetition always carries a difference within it. David, as we have seen, insists that an exact repetition is possible when he narrates the events surrounding Ham's and Steerforth's deaths. But other experiences, particularly the failure of his first marriage, will lead David to question the possibility of exact repetition.

The hostility which realism directs toward a differential vision of language is, as I suggested above, a hostility to time. If there is a difference between the word and the thing, then the word marks the place of the thing's absence. Where the word is, the thing once was. The word re-presents the thing in the present, but the thing itself is lost. Difference is loss—and if only the word, not the thing, can be called to presence, the difference is not only loss, but death. What cannot be repeated is dead. The narrative is obsessed with the fleeting nature of all experience, especially moments of happiness. One of the most perfect moments in the novel is the happy scene following Emily's acceptance of Ham, a scene interrupted by David and Steerforth entering Mr. Peggotty's boat. As David finishes describing the scene, he adds: "The little picture was so instantaneously dissolved by our going in, that one might have doubted whether it had ever been." The brute facts of time and change, carrying the message of death (whose symbol is the sea), seem to overwhelm all human constructions. Peggotty's boat is a refuge from the sea, but it is destroyed in the storm which kills Ham and Steerforth. The dissolution of that happy scene points toward the larger dissolutions in the novel; the narrative can only reconstitute the scene in words. Words can never die, can always be said again, but things and situations do not enjoy the same immunity to time.

The child, in a world of immediate perception, also lives in a world of an eternal present. "As to any sense of inequality, or youthfulness, or other difficulty in our way, little Em'ly and I had no such trouble, because we had no future. We made no more provision for growing older, than we did for growing younger." Realism wants to restore the child's world, resenting language for its destruction of the world in which all there is is completely present; language introduces a world in which reality is dispersed over time and space, with only a small fragment of the totality present to us in any particular moment. Most of reality is only present to us in words which represent absent objects. The eternal and full present of the child is lost, and mourned.

Both the psychologist and the theologian will recognize the narrative's presentation of that loss. The child loses his mother, and is expelled from a garden "where the fruit clusters on the trees, riper and richer than fruit has ever been since, in any other garden." David's first marriage must be seen as an attempt to regain this lost paradise, with Dora slated to play the role of the lost mother. (In Hablot K. Browne's illustration of David's meeting with Dora at her aunts' house, a copy of *Paradise Regained* is prominently displayed on the book shelf.) But a repetition of that earlier happiness is impossible, and David comes to admit, uneasily to be sure, that loss is inevitable. "What I missed, I still regarded—I always regarded—as something that had been a dream of my youthful fancy; that was incapable of realisation; that I was now discovering to be so, with some natural pain, as all men did." The "disciplined" David gives up the "dream of . . . youthful fancy" that time and death can be overcome, accepting Agnes, the bride whose habitual gesture of "pointing upward" links her with a peaceful acceptance of death. But the dream of a perfect and eternal present is not renounced without suggesting that life is a prison. Describing the death of his and Dora's child, David writes: "The spirit fluttered for a moment on the threshold of its little prison, and, unconscious of captivity, took wing." Imprisoned in time, men are barred from eternal union with the dearest objects of perception.

Once the historical nature of experience is accepted, language is not only necessary, but can be recognized as the source of many benefits. Even if words do, at times, confuse rather than clarify, they alone make meaning possible. The child David sees Murdstone's visits to his mother, but remains completely innocent of their meaning. "No such thing came into my mind or near it. I could observe, in little pieces, as it were; but as to making a net of a number of these pieces, and catching anybody in it, that was, as yet, beyond me." Immediate perception is always of "little pieces" because it only registers what is present. Meaning can only be grasped when the connections between disparate events are explored; most of these events are, necessarily, no longer perceptually available. Language is the "net" in which the various pieces supplied by perception are caught and put together. Words grant us access to absent events, particularly events distanced in time from the present.

The limits of sight, which is the child's only reliance, are evidenced in David's inability to see anything through the telescope. The child, living in the present, is unable to use his past to discover patterns which would allow him to understand what is about to happen in the future. His exile in the present means that his perception of its objects is especially intense and particularly innocent, but his understanding of the present's relation to a whole sequence of events, by which its meaning is constituted, is limited.

Language also grants the ability to share these grasped meanings with others, to make significance available to a community. The whole subplot of the Strongs' marriage makes this point: open statements of one's feelings form the basis of love and community. David learns the same lesson in his courtship and marriage of Dora. His secret engagement only leads to trouble, while his openness with Dora's aunts makes the marriage possible. Once married, he is oppressed by all the things he cannot talk about with his wife. "That it would have been better for me if my wife could have helped me more, and shared the many thoughts in which I had no partner; and that this might have been; I knew." The community established by language is an important consolidation for what has been lost in entering the realm of language, of history. David's narrative tries to create with the reader that ideal openness of expression which he also achieves in his second marriage. Since the experiences of individuals vary, only language can establish a community in which one can share what has been present to him by representing it in words to another.

Furthermore, and this is the crucial point, in representation, in the repetition of his history in the "now" of writing, David can discover its significance. When the past is relived and memory used to recognize the present's novelty (its difference), the "mistaken impulses" of the past can be overcome. Aunt Betsey sums up the novel's whole message concerning repetition and memory when she states: "It's in vain, Trot, to recall the past, unless it works some influence upon the present." The difference between the original and its repetition is a saving difference, one that is not to be lamented. Realistic, exact repetition is obsessional, leaving no room for growth or progress; repetition with a difference is liberating. David's fear of exact repetition is apparent in his reaction to the story of Lazarus; he does not want the resurrection of the dead, but only the memory of the dead. His father's tombstone is a comforting and significant monument in the child's world, but a returned father is a terrifying thought. In more obvious cases David does not as readily admit his desire that the past remain dead except in memory. (As I have noted, at times he explicitly desires the opposite.) But even while regretting his mother's fate, David's narrative shows his becoming reconciled to the fact of loss, learning to accept the substitutes time offers him. David writes: "how blest I was in having such a friend in Steerforth, such a friend as Peggotty, and such a substitute for what I had lost as my excellent and generous aunt."

French psychoanalyst Jacques Lacan has noted the movement from object to object in the "chain of desire," each object existing as a substitute for (as a signifier of) the original lost object, generally the mother. For Lacan, repetition is both inevitable and impossible: inevitable in that we always focus our desires on objects which recall the original object; impossible because the original object will never return and never be replaced. This movement of desire is precipitated by our continual reinterpretation of our desires; only this ability to revise our desires moves us from one object to another. Neurosis is defined as obsessive fixation on a particular object, as acute nostalgia. (By this definition, David's love for Dora is neurotic.) Therapy functions to aid the patient's movement from one object to another; in therapy the patient repeats his past not only in the narration of old memories but also in the transference relationship, and through this repetition is able to reinterpret the past and form new desires on the basis of this reinterpretation.

The relevance of this account to *David Copperfield* is clear. David must accept the fact of loss and the substitute time offers him. Comedy is possible when a writer is able to affirm this process of substitution, is able to affirm the changes time brings and the various new objects he desires. (We should note that these new objects function as words, since they are always not only themselves but also signs of the original object. Thus the new objects always carry the mark of difference, of death, since they remind us of the loss of the original object even while consoling us for that loss.) This affirmation requires the renunciation of realism (the insistence that the representative *be* the thing) and implies the acceptance of difference, of death. Time offers new possibilities to the novel's hero, but these can be seized only if he is reconciled to living in situations which are not the same as those of his past. Language becomes crucially important because it is the field of reinterpretation, the space in which that which is similar yet different appears and allows the movement away from the lost past. Words, in their difference from things, necessarily change the world in the act of representing it.

The Strongs' marriage offers a minor instance of this crucial act of reinterpretation. When Dr. Strong says: "Much that I have seen, but not noted, has come back upon me with new meaning," he echoes a very similar statement made earlier by David: "And now, I must confess, the recollection of what I had seen on that night when Mr. Maldon went away, first began to return upon me with a meaning it had never had, and to trouble me." The Strongs' difficulties point out the dangers of misinterpretation and also indicate that the significance of the past is not fixed, but altered by the understanding of it developed in the present.

David's narrative recognizes the special role that stories and art play in this task of reinterpretation. After the first time he ever goes to the theater, David is "filled with the play, and with the past—for it was, in a manner, like a shining transparency, through which I saw my earlier life moving along." The play's ability to cause him to recall the past is in no way linked to any resemblance between it (he has seen *Julius Caesar*) and that past, but, it would seem, results from the play's existence in a realm a step removed from reality. Memory takes place in time, but it is also a way of stepping back from complete immersion in the present. Art stands in a similar relation to the present, and seems to invite David to run his eye over the whole of his experience. And the state of mind produced by the play gives David the "confidence," which "at another time [he] might have wanted," to speak to Steerforth when he sees him that night at the hotel.

Stories not only evoke the past but point toward a future as well. From his childhood readings, David derives "visions" of other times and places which appear "as if they were faintly painted or written on the wall" of his room. In the retreat from time (even while it is within time) which is the space of art, the future, as well as the past, can be written. And it is this writing that David's narrative of his "personal history" undertakes.

A more direct liberation into the future by way of story is David's repetition, while working in the warehouse, "again, and again, and a hundred times again . . . [of] that old story" of his birth and Aunt Betsey's part in it. He focuses on his mother's belief that his aunt had touched her hair "with no ungentle hand," a belief which "might have been altogether my mother's fancy, and might have had no foundation whatever in fact." However, as Dickens will insist throughout the 1850s, this element of fancy is precisely what makes stories liberating. Whether this part of the story is true or not, the reader never discovers; it is enough to know that David acts upon that interpretation, running away to Dover—and that this "fancy" is repeated after his arrival. "It might have been a dream, originating in the fancy which had occupied my mind so long, but I awoke with the impression that my aunt had come and bent over me, and had put my hair away from my face, and laid my head more comfortably, and had then stood looking at me. The words, 'Pretty fellow,' or 'Poor fellow,' seemed to be in my ears, too; but certainly there was nothing else, when I awoke, to lead me to believe that they had been uttered by my aunt, who sat in the bow-window gazing at the sea." Whether this incident is fact or fancy is irrelevant to its allowing another interpretation of Aunt Betsey's character, one which gives David hope, and which furnishes support for his new beginning.

Aunt Betsey insists that the past must be recalled to influence the present when relating her own "past history," finding in her neglect of David's parents a reason to aid him. Part of David's recovery after Dora's death is attributed to his writing a semiautobiographical story. When reinterpretation and the acceptance of substitutes for the desired objects of the past are affirmed, writing and its ability to represent, to repeat, are also affirmed. David fluctuates between accepting the difference inherent in writing and its repetition and struggling to overcome that difference to "see" his past as if it were present. At times, this fluctuation results in an appreciation of fancy which looks forward to the fifties, but at other times it leads to a characterization of fancy as childish that is worthy of Mr. Gradgrind. Fancy is aligned with difference, and the narrative cannot lose its suspicion that reinterpretations are in some way unreal and, as unreal, are just words, not a very good consolation for the lost object.

David's uneasiness with the place of fancy leaves the most complete demonstration of the power of the word to Mr. Micawber. In his denunciation of Uriah Heep, Micawber, characteristically, depends on language to provide him with the energy necessary to carry out his arduous task. The name Heep, repeated time and again, carries within it all the reasons for Micawber's activities, and is called upon whenever he requires fresh inspiration. David describes Micawber's reliance on the word: "With this last repetition of the magic word that had kept him going at all, and in which he surpassed all his previous efforts, Mr. Micawber rushed out of the house." By a significant displacement, Micawber is able to practice the repetition which David is uneasy about, and by means of that repetition Micawber causes Heep's downfall and the Wickfields' liberation, a feat the novel's hero has been unable to effect. In Micawber the narrative recognizes the necessity of repetition, even while remaining unable to endorse it unconditionally or to recognize explicitly its own act of repeating in words the narrator's past.

The word in art, in repetition, is magic; by merely talking about it the past can be changed, a change which must also influence the present. This is the basis of the "talking cure" developed by Freud; a reevaluation of the past in words can successfully cure the patient's present illness. Literature often demonstrates its faith in a similar magic; it is not surprising that Dickens should examine this possibility in a novel in which he was writing about a past he had long kept repressed. In union with an audience who will endorse his transforming words—the readers to whom the novel appeals in its opening sentence—the writer can change the world. In *David Copperfield,* Dickens is shy of this power, afraid that the writer's changes are "fanciful," but in subsequent years, as his disillusionment with the "real" England grows, he will rely more and more on"fancy" as an escape from that England, and as a possible means of changing it.

# Mr. Peggotty and Little Em'ly: Misassessed Altruism?

*Philip M. Weinstein*

It is hard not to see in the denouement of [David and Dora's] marriage a shadowy repetition of the denouement of Clara Murdstone's marriage. There a cold disciplinarian tampered with a loving child-wife until he broke her heart and she died. Here, a gentle disciplinarian tampers briefly with his loving child-wife, pulls back in horror at his behavior, is stalemated. At this point the *deus ex machina* descends, and—no gentle disciplinarian he—does the requisite dirty work. David is putatively disciplined, but the plot surreptitiously inflicts the real discipline on Dora. She is stricken with a mysterious mortal disease, and David is permitted to escape from his prison, with his highminded idealism still intact, free to marry Agnes. In each case the insufficiently loved woman *does* die, but only in the earlier case is blame ascribed. Given the way David both applies an inadequate notion of discipline and is simultaneously released from the price of its application, it is difficult to see his relationship with Dora as a persuasive study in successful self-control. Such confusions attain their acme in the most egregiously misassessed altruistic relationship in the novel, that between Mr. Peggotty and Little Em'ly.

Not accidentally, David and Steerforth burst in upon the Peggotty home at the portentous moment when Emily's engagement to Ham is being announced. Announced, however, not by Ham—who is rarely articulate—but by Mr. Peggotty. And it turns out that Mr. Peggotty has also done Ham's proposing for him: "Well! I counsels him to speak to Em'ly. He's

From *The Semantics of Desire: Changing Models of Identity from Dickens to Joyce*.

big enough, but he's bashfuller than a little un, and he don't like. So *I* speak." The scene that unfolds is massively dominated by Mr. Peggotty. Neither his niece nor his nephew initiates now, nor initiated earlier, any proposition. Instead, Ham and Emily have courted each other through the old man, as he negotiated Ham's wavering offer and Emily's initial refusal, and finally ratified her acceptance. He coordinates, narrates, and registers the emotional significance of their courtship. We cannot but perceive it as *his* courtship.

The upshot is that, while the nominal fiancé is Ham, the scene is so imagined by Dickens and conveyed to the reader that the voice of overriding affection belongs to Mr. Peggotty. All troths are plighted to him. An underlying logic in the novel almost requires that the male most profoundly betrayed by Steerforth should be Peggotty, not Ham. The pattern resonates: the first David Copperfield, Wickfield, Dr. Strong, Mr. Peggotty are all older men uneasily doubling as fathers and husbands. Unable to abandon or endorse this fantasy-desire, Dickens insistently shadows these father / husbands with their potential betrayers: Murdstone, Heep, Maldon, and Steerforth.

Whether it reflects his unquenched feeling for the adolescent Mary Hogarth or some other blockage in his imaginative makeup that prevents him from providing his young heroines with sexual partners their own age—whatever the reason, Dickens is obsessed (as many critics have noted) with the older man playing this double role. One may hazard that the screen afforded by the doubleness appealed to his imagination. As ostensible father, the older man nobly transcends those passions which, as latent lover, he may surreptitiously indulge. Successfully mislabeled, his passion bypasses awareness and can be released without hindrance. Old Peggotty is the extreme instance of a figure whose milder incarnations include Nell's grandfather, John Jarndyce, Arthur Clennam, Joe Gargery, and Eugene Wrayburn. (One of the many reasons why the unfinished *Mystery of Edwin Drood* marks a further stage in Dickens's art is that finally, in John Jasper, parental benevolence and erotic obsession are eerily and [on Dickens's part] consciously fused. He seems to have recognized what he had been suggesting all along: that Quilp and Nell's grandfather are two facets of the same psyche.) Dickens's imagination finds this configuration alternately menacing and seductive; the younger man may appear as either a rescuer or a betrayer. The constant is the scenario itself.

Only after Emily runs off with Steerforth does the old man's double identity become clamorous. We see that if he is ostensibly a father, he is more profoundly a betrayed lover. His extraordinary design—to track her down and bring her back—is instantaneously adopted and embarked on:

> "I'm a going to seek her, fur and wide. If she should come home while I'm away,—but ah, that ain't like to be!—or if I should bring her back, my meaning is, that she and me shall live and die where no one can't reproach her. If any hurt should come to me, remember that the last words I left for her was, 'My unchanged love is with my darling child, and I forgive her!' "

When Faulkner's Quentin wishes he could flee with Caddy and "isolate her out of the loud world" of experience, the wish is explicitly identifiable as a fantasy of incest and escape. Mr. Peggotty's scenario is equally pathological, though never so assessed. The entire world gets reduced in it to a hiding ground for Emily; and the world's inhabitants are reduced to himself as forgiving God, Emily as errant creature, all others as helpful, harmful, or indifferent spectators. (Mr. Peggotty's descriptions to David of his journeys throughout Europe in search of Emily bear the mark of rampant fantasy. Cf. the following: " 'By little and little, when I come to a new village or that, among the poor people, I found they know'd about me. They would set me down at their cottage-doors, and give me what-not fur to eat and drink, and show me wheer to sleep; and many a woman, Mas'r Davy, as has had a daughter of about Em'ly's age, I've found a-waiting for me, at Our Saviour's Cross outside the village, fur to do me sim'lar kindnesses. Some has had daughters as was dead. And God only knows how good them mothers was to me!' " The passage is shaped, not by the requirements of plausibility, but by those of a fantasized universe of loving parents and lost children. It reminds one of Blake's poems of lost children in the *Songs of Innocence*.) As Q. D. Leavis says, "While Mr. Peggotty seems at first sight to offer the pattern of disinterested devotion to the winning child he had fostered, what emerges is a horribly possessive love that is expressed characteristically in heat, violence and fantasies, impressing us as maniacal." (Leavis differs from me in believing that Dickens knows what he is doing here, and that the portrait of Peggotty is meant to express "morbid states and the strange self-deceptions of human nature." If Freudian diction be permitted, rarely has the id more spectacularly passed itself off as the superego.

Incisively, Dickens juxtaposes Peggotty's suspect sweetness toward Emily against Rosa Dartle's authentic anger. This passage occurs one page before Peggotty's just quoted speech and nicely silhouettes it:

> "I would have her whipped! . . . I would have her branded on the face, drest in rags, and cast out in the streets to starve. If I had the power to sit in judgment on her, I would see it done.

> See it done? I would do it! . . . If I could hunt her to the grave, I would. If there was any word of comfort that would be a solace to her in her dying hour, and only I possessed it, I wouldn't part with it for Life itself."

Excessive, we say to ourselves, and indeed her words are insanely vindictive. They carry anger without alloy, just as Peggotty's claim to carry forgiveness without alloy. The imaginative wholeness of the novel—its elaborate network of covert single hands and interconnected "nervous ganglia" [in Dorothy Van Ghent's phrase]—surreptitiously join both responses, showing them to be mirrors of each other, both actuated—one entirely, the other in part—by ferocious jealousy. Thus when Emily is finally found, Dickens permits Peggotty to rescue her only after Rosa Dartle has administered a tongue-lashing so corrosive and elaborate that it fills up four pages of text.

Inexplicably, David remains hidden and silent; he refuses to interfere. In a sympathetic attempt to justify David's behavior in the novel, Janet Brown points to this scene and claims that the reader accepts David's passivity: "He is to be present, that is all. He is prepared for nothing more." Nevertheless, she concedes that his silence imposes "an outrageously unjust penalty on Emily."

What seems clear is that Dickens *is* granting Rosa the "power" she requested: "to sit in judgment on her . . . See it done? I would do it!" When she is finished doing it, having reduced Emily to a quivering mass of repentance, Peggotty is finally allowed to enter:

> "Uncle!"
>
> A fearful cry followed the word. I paused a moment, and looking in, saw him supporting her insensible figure in his arms. He gazed for a few seconds in the face, then stooped to kiss it—oh, how tenderly!—and drew a handerchief before it.
>
> "Mas'r Davy," he said, in a low tremulous voice, when it was covered, "I thank my Heav'nly Father as my dream's come true! I thank Him hearty for having guided me, in His own ways, to my darling!"

"His own ways" is a rich phrase. Insofar as we are meant to assent to it—and the corroborative context sugggests that we are—it conveys Dickens's attempt to assess the treatment of Emily in his culture's terms of Christian forgiveness. It serves, as well, as a screen for inadmissible, passionate motives. "His own ways" involve a blistering attack upon Emily, a full venting of outrage at her sexual misconduct. This anger, once expressed in the narrative design of the novel, however, is scrupulously ignored by David, Peggotty, and Dickens. It is passed off as a mere irrelevance in a larger scenario that is labeled divinely beneficent. Emily is indeed forgiven, but the form of forgiveness—a corrosive tongue-lashing followed by permanent exile with Peggotty—serves also as a disguised punishment for Emily, an illicit reward for Peggotty. (The scene was on first conception even stranger. In the manuscript version Dickens actually has Peggotty accompany David to the room in which Rosa is lambasting Emily. When David is moved by pity to intervene, Peggotty forcibly holds him back. The manuscript concludes: "Mr. Peggotty waited until she [Rosa] was gone, as if his duty were too sacred to be discharged in such a presence, and then passed into the room." There is reason to believe that Dickens scented the perverse odor emanating from Peggotty's behavior here: within the week that intervened between the manuscript version and the printed galleys for this number, he decided massively to revise the episode. He simply removed Peggotty from the encounter until the very end, thereby attenuating David's motive for passivity but, more importantly, keeping Peggotty's high-mindedness intact. Still, the jealousy / outrage motives are deep-seated and ineradicable; they manage to surface even in the revised scene, and they are manifest elsewhere.)

Once he has found Emily, old Peggotty takes further steps to realize his fantasy. Australia now enters the novel as the never-never land where what fails in England is finally granted success. When David asks Peggotty if he and Emily are going to Australia "quite alone," he is told:

> "Aye, Mas'r Davy!" he returned. "My sister, you see, she's that fond of you and yourn . . . that it wouldn't be hardly fair to let her go. Besides which, theer's one she has in charge, Mas'r Davy, as doen't ought to be forgot."
>
> "Poor Ham!" said I.
>
> "My good sister takes care of his house . . . and he takes kindly to her . . . He'll set and talk to her, with a calm spirit, wen it's like he couldn't bring himself to open his lips to another. Poor fellow! . . . theer's not so much left him, that he could spare the little as he has!"

The talk moves to Mrs. Gummidge; Peggotty explains his plans for taking care of her as well; and David reflects: "He forgot nobody. He thought of everybody's claims and strivings, but his own." His own "claims and strivings," I hope it is clear by now, are supremely well served. The "love unknown to earth" that David fantasized over with respect to Agnes is granted to Peggotty in Australia. In having his Little Em'ly to himself, he has what he wants: the stunning instance of a man whose claims and strivings are forgotten is not Peggotty but his nephew Ham.

The emotional dynamics involved in this obscure trade-off can only be guessed at. Emily's stain in effect kills off Ham and rejuvenates Peggotty. As fallen woman, Emily cannot be married; for any legitimate lover she is "damaged goods." For an unadmitted lover, however, she is now available, all implicit charges of Peggotty's selfishness being annulled by her stain. She is perfectly free, and only free, to live an exiled life with a father-figure now doubling as a husband-figure. So the old man's sister moves to the waning young man, and the young man's fiancée moves to the vigorous old man. That Peggotty could in good conscience thus replace his nephew, that Ham could be as resolutely and unresistingly killed off as Dora was—these fantastic transactions characterize an imaginative world in which "His own ways" are Dickensian but hardly godlike; that is, they are anything but persuasively disciplined, unified, and altruistic.

# Secret Subjects, Open Secrets

*D. A. Miller*

> *"And who's this shaver?" said one of the gentlemen, taking hold of me.*
> *"That's Davy," returned Mr Murdstone.*
> *"Davy who?" said the gentleman.*

For a moment in *David Copperfield*, the text raises the possibility that David might be any David; for a moment, it so happens, it invites me to imagine that he might be myself. Assuming that autobiographical representation is replete with such narcissistic lures, sites where the reader's own subjectivity comes to be invoked and identified, even without benefit of a namesake, why not begin with myself? Why not begin by recounting the insertion of my own person into a novel which I read and reread as a child, "in those tender years," Virginia Woolf called them, "when fact and fiction merge"? Why not anthologize those all-too-affecting passages in the novel through which David's story—I mean the other one's—became hopelessly entangled with my own? Why not admit, by the way, how readily everything else in this novel flees from my memory—rather, how peremptorily everything else is dismissed from it: much as the other David admits, sitting by the fire, that "there was nothing real in all that I remembered, save my mother, Peggotty, and I"? And why not gloss those figures in the novel who have signified and predicted my sentimental education: from the Mother who fondled me, saying "Davy, my pretty boy! my poor child!"; the (step-) Father whose unfeeding hand I rabidly bit; the Friend who, though Mr. Sharp and Mr. Mell were notable personages in my eyes, was to them what the sun was to two stars; and the (second) Wife, center and circle of my life, in whom I might have inspired a dearer love; down to David himself,

From *Dickens Studies Annual* 14 (1985). 

cognate and first cognition of myself, who, of a summer evening, the boys at play in the churchyard, sat on my bed, reading as if for life.

But as I eagerly put these questions, in the arrogant rhetorical form that waited for no reply, but already did what it pretended to ask permission for, I was also obliged to recognize why, "subduing my desire to linger yet," I must not pursue such a confession. For we are all well acquainted with those mortifying charges (sentimentality, self-indulgence, narcissism) which our culture is prepared to bring against anyone who dwells in subjectivity longer or more intensely than is necessary to his proper functioning as the agent of socially useful work. (It is bad enough to tell tales out of school, but to tell them in school— or what comes to the same, in a text wholly destined for the academy—would be intolerable.) And those envious charges have at least this much truth in them, that the embarrassing risk of *being too personal* all too often comes to coincide with its opposite in the dismal fate of banality, of *not being personal enough*. Nothing, for instance, is more striking than the disproportion between the embarrassed subject and the occasion of his embarrassment: while the former imagines his subjectivity on conspicuous and defenseless display, the latter has usually been rendered all but invisible by its sheer mundaneness, its cultural or physiological predictability. Rarely does anyone even think to watch the spectacle we assumed we were making of ourselves. We say truly, "I could have died of embarrassment," but nearer than one's fantasized murder at the hands (the eyes, the tongues) of the others is the danger lest such worldly homicide prove embarrassingly unnecessary, the subject who fears extinction having already died out on his own. The painfulness of embarrassment, which at least ought to have guaranteed its subject's vitality, instead betokens a mountainously agitated subjectivity which refuses to acknowledge its mousey stillbirths. Accordingly, what could whatever "embarrassed" revelations I might make about my intimacy with *David Copperfield* amount to, except a particularly cathected paraphrase of an already written text? What could I—presumptively unique, private subject of unique, private desires—finally signify in such revelations, but a character in a novel so familiar that no one, it is said, can even remember reading it for the first time?

Let me not, then, speak of myself, but let my seduction by *David Copperfield* stay a secret. Yet is my secrecy any less paradoxical than the embarrassment that I thereby seem to avoid? It almost goes without saying that, though I conceal the details of this seduction, they would not be very difficult to surmise: no more esoteric, perhaps, than Oedipus and his commonplace complex. For I have had to intimate my secret, if only *not to tell it*; and conversely, in theatrically continuing to keep my secret, I have already rather *given it away*. But if I don't tell my secret, why can't I keep it better? And if I can't keep it better, why don't I just tell it? I can't quite tell my secret, because then it would be known that there was nothing really special to hide, and no one really special to hide it. But I can't quite keep it either, because then it would not be believed that there *was* something to hide and someone to hide it. It is thus a misleading common sense that finds the necessity of secrecy in the "special" nature of the contents concealed, when all that revelation usually reveals is a widely diffused cultural prescription, a cliché. A character in Oscar Wilde is closer to the truth when he observes of secrecy that "it is the one thing that can make modern life mysterious and marvellous. The commonest thing is delightful if one only hides it." More precisely, secrecy would seem to be a mode whose ultimate meaning lies in the subject's formal insistence that he is radically inaccessible to the culture that would otherwise entirely determine him. I cannot, therefore, resolve the double bind of a secrecy which must always be rigorously maintained in the face of a secret that everybody already knows, since this is the very condition that entitles me to my subjectivity in the first place. But the double bind is not at all the same thing as a dead end, and if I cannot speak of myself without losing myself in the process, I can keep myself secret and—"so to speak"— change the subject: convinced of my indeterminableness in the safety of silence, as I speak of—and seek to determine—somebody or something else. Were not the personal rewards for good behavior in the administered society so readily accepted, it might seem strange that I can best establish myself as a private subject only in the dutiful performance of the professional obligation that it profits nothing to put off any longer: to speak of *David Copperfield*.

We begin, then, not with myself, but with the first paragraph of Dickens's text, which falls in his preface:

> I do not find it easy to get sufficiently far away from this Book, in the first sensations of having finished it, to refer to it with the composure which this formal heading would seem to require. My interest in it, is so recent and strong; and my mind is so divided between pleasure and regret—pleasure in the achievements of a long design, regret in the separation from many companions—that I am in danger of wearying the reader whom I love, with personal confidences and private emotions.

Strongly hinting at the intimate and specular nature of his relationship to *David Copperfield*, Dickens nonetheless courteously refrains from elaborating on it. Yet it is fair to wonder how "wearying" the personal confidences and private emotions could possibly be, when something very like them has been appetizingly promised on the title page of the very book that Dickens is presenting: "The Personal History, Adventures, Experience, & Observation of David Copperfield . . . (Which He never meant to be Published on any Account)." And if we do not fully believe in their wearisomeness, neither can we quite credit the "love" for the reader on whose account they are suppressed: the concern for the burdened reader is surely more defensive than protective. In any event, no sooner is Dickens's subjectivity put before us than it is also put away: made to vanish in the act of proffering the Book itself: "all that I could say of the Story, to any purpose, I have endeavoured to say in it." Unwilling to speak of himself, Dickens instead points to his story of the other, in which C. D., authorial signature, will be inverted—or rather, extroverted—into D. C., sign of a character who is also, as though to indicate his purely verbal existence, sign of a book.

While it may be the usual task of a preface to manage such transitions from author to text, from subjectivity to its eclipse in the object at hand, here, at any rate, the business is not just routine. For the gesture made in Dickens's preface is repeated within the novel by David himself, who regularly and almost ritually "secretes" his subjectivity at precisely what would appear to be its determining moments. For example, when David returns home on holiday from school, he has the more than pleasant surprise of finding his mother alone nursing her newly delivered child:

> I spoke to her, and she stared, and cried out. But seeing me, she called me her dear Davy, her own boy! and coming half across the room to meet me, kneeled down upon the ground and kissed me, and laid my head down on her bosom near the little creature that was nestling there, and put its hand to my lips.
>
> I wish I had died. I wish I had died then, with that feeling in my heart! I should have been more fit for Heaven than I ever have been since.

The supreme importance of the incident seems to depend wholly on the intensity of an affect which, though cited, is never specified. No doubt we could be more precise than David about the nature of that feeling in his heart, whose principal component it would not be hard to nominate: the bliss of recovering the mother in a relationship which has been unexpectedly de-triangulated not only by Murdstone's absence, but also by the presence of the new sibling, a minorized third who is more David's surrogate at the maternal breast than his rival. To which one could add: the unholy excitement at seeing the mother who abandoned him for another abjectly repentant at his feet, along with the already pitiable infant by whom he might have been supplanted a second time; and finally the consequent guilt that accedes to conscience only as the self-satisfied wish to have died in such a state of grace. Yet what matters more than the availability of these determinations is the fact that, even in this ample autobiography, intended for no one's eyes but his own, David only alludes to the feeling whose decisiveness he nevertheless advertises. And much as, in the preface, Dickens managed his own fraught subjectivity by introducing the novel in its place, so David, shortly after this episode, finds himself in his room, "pouring over a book."

The same pattern is enacted in Steerforth's bedroom, to which David "belongs," at Salem House:

> The greater part of the guests had gone to bed as soon as the eating and drinking were over; and we, who had remained whispering and listening half-undressed, at last betook ourselves to bed, too.
>
> "Good night, young Copperfield," said Steerforth. "I'll take care of you."
>
> "You're very kind," I gratefully returned. "I am very much obliged to you."
>
> "You haven't got a sister, have you?" said Steerforth yawning.
>
> "No," I answered.
>
> "That's a pity," said Steerforth. "If you had had one, I should think she would have been a pretty, timid, little, bright-eyed sort of girl. I should have liked to know her. Good night, young Copperfield."
>
> "Good night, sir," I replied.
>
> I thought of him very much after I went to bed, and raised myself, I recollect, to look at him where he lay in the moonlight, with his handsome face turned up, and his head reclining easily on his arm. He was a person of great power in my eyes; that was, of course, the reason of my mind running on him. No veiled future dimly glanced upon him in the moonbeams. There was no shadowy picture of his footsteps, in the garden that I dreamed of walking in all night.

Here again a powerful affect is evoked, but evacuated of any substantial content. *What* did David think of Steerforth as he looked at him where he lay in the moonlight, his handsome face turned up? In one sense, the question scarcely merits an answer, so eloquently here does the love that dare not speak its name speak its metonyms (the "whispering and listening half-undressed," and so on). Yet in another sense, such an answer is positively averted, since David lapses into distractingly cryptic reverie at just the point where—but for the veil of "no veiled future . . ."—the classic erotics of the scene would have become manifest. And once again, the affect is soon displaced in an experience of fiction: in lieu of the nocturnal sexual episode that—as David might say, "of course"—does not take place between him and Steerforth, they organize the institution of bedtime stories, in which David recounts to Steerforth from memory the novels he has read at home. As in the scene with his mother, David's reticence here may be largely "unconscious," but the distinction is secondary to a pattern which is also capable of being rehearsed quite consciously, as when David is forced to do manual labor at Murdstone and Grinby's warehouse. "I never said, to man or boy, how it was that I came to be there, or gave the least indication that I was sorry I was there. That I suffered in secret, and that I suffered exquisitely, no one ever knew but I. How much I suffered, it is . . . utterly beyond my power to tell." The importance of this secret suffering—not just for David, but for Dickens, too, with his own traumatically secreted *déclassement* in Warren's Blacking Factory as a child—is in no danger of being underrated. It only loses the privilege that we are accustomed to accord to it by displaying the common structure of all such important moments in the novel: first the allusion ("how much I suffered . . ."), then the elision (". . . is beyond my power to tell"), and finally the turn to the novelistic, as David attempts to entertain his fellow-workers "with some results of the old readings."

The pattern which thus recurs in David's life, however, finds its most extensive embodiment in his life-story. We notice, for instance, that the gestures of secretiveness are made, not just then, at the time of the narrative ("That I suffered in secret, no one ever knew"), but now as well, at the time of its narration ("How much I suffered, it is beyond my power to tell"). The diffidence of this narration obviously perpetuates the same fears of discipline that inhibited David with the Murdstones, at Salem House (even Steerforth is likened to a magistrate), and in the warehouse. But the narration of this diffidence also perpetuates that turn to (reading, recounting, writing) stories which was David's regular escape from these fears. The manuscript to which, in his own phrase, he *commits his secrets*, is precisely that: the place where he encrypts them. The manuscript to which, in his own phrase, he commits his secrets, *if he knows them*, is rather the place where he encrypts them so as neither to know them nor to make them known. Writing the self, then, would be consistently ruled by the paradoxical proposition that the self is most itself at the moment when its defining inwardness is most secret, most withheld from writing—with the equally paradoxical consequence that autobiography is most successful only where *it has been abandoned for the Novel*. The paradoxes determine not only David, who intimates his subjectivity only to displace it into various modes of experiencing the Novel, but also Dickens, who, just as he abandoned what thus remained an autobiographical fragment to write *David Copperfield* in the first place, strikes, and then strikes out, the personal note in his preface. And what had been, it seemed, my own personal note would now prove no less impersonal than a faithful reproduction of these same paradoxes. Even at the moment of its annunciation, my subjectivity had already been annulled as a mere effect of its object. Or alternatively: I have been able to be a subject in the only way this object-text allows: by pointing to the Novel, where one's own secret will be kept because somebody else's will be revealed. In the knowledge, then, that at least where *David Copperfield* is concerned autobiography can *only* be an "autobiographical fragment," let us again change the subject.

## II

Characters in *David Copperfield* are frequently coupled with boxes: bags, parcels, luggage. Betsey Trotwood can be accurately identified by David, who has never seen her, through the fact that she "carries a bag . . . with a great deal of room in it," and which seems a ready accessory to her "coming down upon you, sharp." Miss Murdstone, who embellishes herself in numerous steel fetters, brings with her to the Rookery "two uncompromising hard black boxes, with her initials on the lids in hard brass nails," and the boxes "were never seen open or known to be left unlocked." Mr. Barkis, himself a carrier of boxes, also has his own, full of money and hidden under his bed, "which he pretended was only full of coats and trousers." So close is the connection between the miser and his box that on his death bed Barkis becomes "as mute and senseless as the box, from which his form derived the only expression it had." As these examples suggest, characters come with boxes because characters come in boxes, as boxes. Some characters in *David Copperfield* run the risk of being put away, in the asylum with which Mr. Dick is threatened or the prison in which Uriah Heep and Littimer are actually incarcerated, and others encounter the fate of being sent away, like David to his room or to school, or even like Jack Maldon, Mr. Mell, the Micawber family, Mr. Peggotty, and Emily, to the colonies, but a far greater number—anticipating an attempting to avert these fates—have simply put themselves away, in boxes that safeguard within their precious subjectivity. Familiar to us as their eccentricities seem to make them, the characters in *David Copperfield* (as though the real function of eccentricity were to render the eccentric a private person, inaccessible to the general) typically manage to be *arcane*—even when they do not literally inhabit, like Daniel Peggotty, an ark.

How do they box themselves in, seal themselves off? At the molecular level of gesture, they may stop up their ears like Betsey Trotwood and Dora, or suck in their cheeks like Uriah Heep, or, like Betsey Trotwood again and Mrs. Markleham, retire behind their fans. At the molar level of deportment, they may take refuge in a militant bearing. The "firmness" recommended and practiced by the Murdstones is not confined to them: it shows up as well in Betsey's "fell rigidity of figure and composure of countenance," in the "atmosphere of respectability" with which Littimer surrounds himself, and in "the outward restraints" that Uriah Heep "puts upon himself." Alternatively, they may pursue a thoroughgoing self-effacement, like Mr. Chillip, who sidles in and out of a room, to take up the less space, or Ham with his "sheepish look," or the "mild" Mr. Mell. Even their dress participates in their self-sequestration. Betsey ties her head up in a handkerchief, and Peggotty throws her apron over her face. Ham wears a pair of such very stiff trousers that they would have stood quite as well alone, and Traddles wears a tight sky-blue suit that made his arms and legs like German sausages. Uriah Heep, like Mr. Spenlow, is "buttoned up to the throat." And when these characters speak, they rarely speak their mind, but more often only its screen: Littimer's composed courtesy, Uriah Heep's hypocritical humility, Betsey's gruff understatement. At the extreme, they protect their subjectivity by refusing to assume it even grammatically: by refusing to say "I," like Markham, who says "a man" instead, or Barkis, who designates himself and his desires in the third person—what, more simply and strictly, Emile Benveniste calls the "non-person."

Thoroughly encased in such diverse armor, the characters in *David Copperfield* prepare to do battle with the outside world. But the battle, fundamentally dubious, has already been lost in the very preparations for it. It is as though the ravages feared from the others have been assumed by the self in its own name, and that the costs of social discipline have been averted only in an equally expensive self-discipline. Part of the expense, surely, is paid out of the moral category which, though frequently and often hysterically invoked by Dickens to differentiate his characters into good ones and bad, proves absolutely irrelevant to the structural uniformity of their self-concealment. No doubt, Uriah Heep's "umbleness" hides only a vaulting ambition and cankering resentment, while Ham's "sheepishness" masks a heroically good nature; and Betsey Trotwood with her bag and her fell rigidity of figure is a quite different moral type from Miss Murdstone with her two black boxes and her firmness. But the obvious moral distinctions here simply overlay a formal similarity of character which they have not determined and are powerless to affect. It is as if Heep and Ham, Betsey Trotwood and Jane Murdstone, however much the ethical content of their inwardness might differ, agreed on the paranoid perception that the social world is a dangerous place to exhibit it, and on the aggressive precautions that must be taken to protect it from exposure. To be good, to be bad are merely variants on the primordial condition which either presupposes: to be *in camera*. Thus, the practical social consequences of goodness, on which Dickens puts strong ideological pressure, are of necessity extremely limited, since the good can only be good, do good, in secret. And the text holds a worse irony in store for the good as well: that in defending against the outrages of socialization, they unwittingly beat them to the punch. Either, to protect themselves against "outside" aggressions, they need to commit them, like Betsey Trotwood stuffing cotton in her ears and then stuffing Ham's ears as well, "as if she confounded them with her own," or later with the donkeys. Or, fearful of the consequences of their aggression, they take it out on themselves, like Mr. Mell, who "would talk to himself sometimes, and grin, and clench his fist, and grind his teeth, and pull his hair in an unaccountable manner." Despite the thin skins in which they are all enveloped (even Murdstone's firm hand can be humiliatingly bitten), characters add to the rough-and-tumble social buffetting from which they would withdraw. Still, if their elaborate defenses finally amount to no more than the fact that they have made their social necessity into their personal choice, this perhaps suffices for a subject who can thus continue to affirm his subjectivity *as a form* even where it no longer has a content of its own.

This is not, of course, the whole story. Such defenses may be indistinguishable from that which they defend against, and thus reduce the subjectivity that mobilizes them to a purely formal category. But they can surely continue to be opposed to that which they defend: the hidden innerness that like the miser's hoard must never see the light of day. Just as we can say of this hoard in a capitalist economy that it is *worth nothing* as soon as it has been removed from circulation and exchange, so we might wonder what value can be put upon an innerness that is never recognized in intersubjectivity. And the epistemological questions inevitably brought forward in such cases are not far away: if the secret subjective content is so well-concealed, how do we know it is there? How does the concealing subject know it is there? What could the content of a subjectivity that is never substantiated possible be? Accordingly, at the same time as the characters in *David Copperfield* embox their subjectivity, they find oblique means and occasions to take the lid off. Peggotty's tendency to burst her buttons, Mr. Mell's pouring what seems like "his whole being" into his doleful flute-playing, the wasting fire within Rosa Dartle finding vent in her gaunt eyes: these are only a few examples of the odd compromises that characters strike, like Freudian hysterics, between expression and repression. In some sense, therefore, the secret subject is always an open secret.

Sometimes, certainly, this open secret is actively *opened*. The dramatic heights of Dickens's fiction are customarily reached when a secret is explosively let out, as at Uriah Heep's unmasking, or when two boxed-in, buttoned-up subjects find release in one another, like David and Peggotty whispering and kissing through the keyhole of his locked room on the last night of his "restraint." Yet even such moments as these only explicate as "information" what had been previously available to characters as "intuition." Though David seems to know Betsey Trotwood only as a legendary dragon, if he nonetheless risks throwing himself on her mercy, sight unseen, it is because he has always known more than this: hadn't his mother told him that "she had a fancy that she felt Miss Betsey touch her hair, and that with no ungentle hand?" Far more often, however, dramatic revelation even of this order is superfluous. Barkis's box might be taken for an emblem of those many secrets in the novel to which everyone is privy: David's "secret" attachment to Dora, which even the drunken dimness of Mrs. Crupp is capable of penetrating; the "secret" of Uriah Heep's interest in Agnes, which he asks others to keep so as to keep them from interfering; Mr. Wickfield's alcoholism, the secret that everyone hides because everyone holds; Miss Murdstone's fetters, "suggesting on the outside, to all beholders, what was to be expected within"; and so on. The radical emptiness of secrecy in the novel is most forcefully (if all unconsciously) argued by Miss Mills, whose "love of the romantic and mysterious" fabricates trivial secrets on the same popular romance principles that make them so easily divined.

Even when a character's subjectivity may be successfully concealed from other characters, for us, readers of the novel, the secret is always out. Like David, we have suspected the good nature that underlies Betsey Trotwood's decided and inflexible exterior, and, long before him, we have detected the "secret" of Agnes's attachment. Similarly, we never doubt that Mr. Mell, mild or unmelodious as a social presence, has the milk of human kindess within; that the Murdstones, despite their firmness, are ultimately purposeless creatures; that Uriah Heep lies through his professions of humility; or that Peggotty is dear and loving for all her comic inarticulateness. The hermeneutic problem put to characters by the discrepancy between outside and inside (such that the former can never be counted on to represent the latter, which it is rather constituted to disguise) is never a problem for us, for whom the outside, riven with expressive vents, quite adequately designates the nature of the subject it thus fails to conceal. For us, all the camouflage that characters devise to deceive one another gives way to readerly transparency, as, no less immediately, their secrets become our sure knowledge.

Yet, curiously enough, the fact that the secret is always known—and, in some obscure sense, known to be known—never interferes with the incessant activity of keeping it. The contradiction does not merely affect characters. We too inevitably surrender our privileged position as readers to whom all secrets are open by "forgetting" our knowledge for the pleasures of suspense and surprise. (Even a first reading, if there is one, is shaped by this obliviscence, which a second makes impossible to doubt.) In this light, it becomes clear that the social function of secrecy—isomorphic with its novelistic function—is not to conceal knowledge, so much as to conceal the knowledge of the knowledge. No doubt an analysis of the kinds of knowledge that it is felt needful to cover in secrecy would tell us much about a given culture or historical period—though in the case of *David Copperfield* the results of such an analysis would be banal in the extreme: sex, drink, and (for the middle-class subject) work are the taboo categories they more or less remain today. But when the game of secrecy is played beyond those contexts that obviously call for suppression, it is evident that the need to "keep secret" takes precedence over whatever social exigencies exist for keeping one or another secret in particular. Instead of the question, "What does secrecy cover?" we had better ask "What covers secrecy?" What, that is, takes secrecy for its field of operations? In a world where the explicit exposure of the subject would manifest how thoroughly he has been inscribed within a socially given totality, secrecy would be the spiritual exercise by which the subject is allowed to conceive of himself as a resistance: a friction in the smooth functioning of the social order, a margin to which its far-reaching discourse does not reach. Secrecy would thus be the subjective practice in which the oppositions of private / public, inside / outside, subject / object are established, and the sanctity of their first term kept inviolate. And the phenomenon of the "open secret" does not, as one might think, bring about the collapse of these binarisms and their ideological effects, but rather attests to their fantasmatic recovery. In a mechanism reminiscent of Freudian disavowal, we know perfectly well that the secret is known, but nonetheless we must persist, however ineptly, in guarding it. The paradox of the open secret registers the subject's accommodation to a totalizing system which has obliterated the difference he would make—the difference he does make, in the imaginary denial of this system "even so."

## III

It remains, therefore, an odd fact that readers have traditionally found the Dickens character, particularly in *David Copperfield,* a source of great "charm." What charm, we may ask, is there in the spectacle of such pathetically reduced beings, maimed by their own defense mechanisms, and whose undoubtedly immense energy can only be expended to fix them all the more irremovably in a total social system? How is it that such grotesques are not perceived as the appalling evidence of what T. W. Adorno, speaking of the fate of the subject in such a system, calls "damaged life," but instead as the complacently enjoyed proof of our own unimpaired ability to love them? The charm we allow to Dickens's characters, I submit, is ultimately no more than the debt of gratitude we pay to their fixity for giving us, in contrast, our freedom. We condescend to praise these characters as "inimitable" because they make manifest how safe we are from the possibility of actually imitating them. The reduced model of the subject which they exemplify is refuted or transcended automatically in any reader's experience. For one thing, the consciousness of this reader, effortlessly capable of disarming their self-betraying defenses and penetrating their well-known secrets, must always thereby exceed that of the characters, both individually and severally. Indeed, this "inclusive" consciousness is part of what contributes to the sense that the characters are boxed in. For another, the novel-reading subject can never resemble Dickens's characters, conspicuously encased yet so transparent that they are always inside-out, because the novel-reading subject as such has no outside. However much this subject inclusively sees, he is never seen in turn, being invisible both to himself (he is reading a novel) and to others (he is reading it in private). The boxed-in characters already so reified that they are easily and frequently likened to things (boxes great, like rooms and houses, as well as small), thus come to play object to the (faceless, solitary, secreted) reading subject, whose structural position and the comparison that reinforces it both release *him* from the conditions that determine *them*.

The reader's comparative freedom vis-à-vis the constraints of character is, of course, a general effect in the nineteenth-century novel. For if the Novel is the genre of "secret singularity," it becomes so less by providing us with an intimate glimpse of a character's inner life than by determining this life in such a way that its limitations must forcibly contrast with our own less specified, less violated inwardness. The contrast is inscribed within the nineteenth-century novel as one between the character and the narrator, our readerly surrogate and point of view, who is in general so shadowy and indeterminate a figure that it scarcely seems right to call him a person at all. But Dickens's fiction is particularly relevant to the problematics of modern subjectivity, because his novels pose such a sharp contrast in the extreme difference and distance between the character, who is so thoroughly extroverted that his inner life seems exiguous, and the narrator, who is so completely defaced that, even when he bears a name like David Copperfield, Phiz hardly knows what "phiz" to give him.

As early as the *Sketches by Boz*, these problematics are already rehearsed, though in ways that *David Copperfield* will modify substantially. Formally speaking, the narrative in the *Sketches* is skimpy, fragmentary, never more than anecdotal: stories either never get off the ground, or if they do, terminate in the arrested development characteristic of the "short story." Thematically speaking, the deficiency of narrative in the text corresponds to the lack of adventure, even as a possibility, in the world the text represents. On one hand, a viable agent of adventure cannot really emerge from among the dwarfed and emaciated subjects (typically too small or too thin) who populate the metropolis and who are far too much like the objects that overwhelm them there. And like the diverse articles inventoried in the various junkshops Boz visits—human products divorced from human production or use—these short, foreshortened subjects are serially juxtaposed to one another without ever forming a cohesive "community." On the other hand, even if a properly qualified agent of adventure did appear—and several characters at least attempt to qualify for the role—his adventure could only be played out as parody in a world which has routinized even the opportunities for breaking routine. (In "Making a Night of It," for example, the carnivalesque release from clerical chores is as regular as the quarterly pay for doing them.) And should routine fail to meet the case, there would always be the police to close it: the police who appear to stand on every London streetcorner and whose function, like that of their many surrogates in the *Sketches*, is to return adventure to the confinement from which it all too briefly emerged.

Yet every dreary characteristic of the world that Boz represents has been overcome in his representation. Though this world is bound in stasis,

Boz is demonstrably the free-ranging flaneur, and to him, in his casual meanderings, befall the adventurous possibilities denied to the characters. Though the world of objects is mute, Boz has wit enough to overcome its alienation and make it speak once more to and of human subjects. And though the faces Boz gazes upon are horribly precise in the deformations by which they reveal class, profession, and the general scars of city-dwelling, Boz himself, faceless, shows none of them. Even the characters' lack of community is negated by Boz's confident use of the plural first-personal pronoun, as though here were a subject who could count on allies. Altogether, it is as if the problems or constraints arising from the dull urbanism of the *Sketches* found their solution or release in the lively urbanity of the sketching.

The very disparity between problem and solution, however, means that the latter must engender certain problems of its own. Insofar as the subject (Boz) and the object (the world he sketches, including its reified subjects) are merely juxtaposed, each pole retaining its own distinctness, the "solution" borne in the narration has no bearing on the "problem" it would solve—except, no doubt, to offer further evidence of it in the mere contiguity of terms that otherwise remain mutually unrecognizable and unrelated. The lack of any interactive or dialectical connection between subject and object thus becomes registered as the fragmentary form of the sketches themselves, which not only bespeaks the inability of the subject to master his materials, whose abiding heterogeneity can be grasped only in bits and pieces, but also casts into the shadow of a doubt the continuity of that very subject, whose freedom is purchased at the price of his intermittence, his utter ungroundedness. The interest of *David Copperfield* in this light is that the two models of subjectivity which the *Sketches* never reconcile—the one objectified in the character, the other abstracted in the narrator—are here linked and mediated in the acutal story, in which a character becomes his own narrator. As Copperfield the narrator recounts the life (really, the death) of David the character, we witness an abstracted, all-embracing subjectivity telling the story of its own genesis, of how, and against what odds and with what at stake, it came to be. Implicitly, the process submits the whole category of the "social" to radical revision. It is not that the phenomenology which (as in *Boz*) locates the social outside the subject is ever abandoned, but rather that, instead of being taken for granted, it now has to be produced. No longer a mere content whose oppressions or determinations are confined to the second term of a rigid opposition between self and other (or between subject and object, or narrator and character), the social now appears as the very field in which these oppositions are strategically constituted.

## IV

We need, then, to consider the story of this autobiography, whose essential drama stems from David's desperate attempt not to be boxed in, or confounded with a box, like the other characters. "Master Copperfield's box there!" says Miss Murdstone, as the wheels of Barkis's cart are heard at the Rookery gates. Her words, as always, are ominous, and at the coaching inn not long afterwards, David has the anxious experience of being abandoned among boxes, as he waits on the luggage scale for someone from Salem House to claim him:

> Here, as I sat looking at the parcels, packages, and books . . . a procession of most tremendous considerations began to march through my mind. Supposing nobody should ever fetch me, how long would they consent to keep me there? Would they keep me long enough to spend seven shillings? Should I sleep at night in one of those wooden bins, with the other luggage, and wash myself at the pump in the yard in the morning; or should I be turned out every night, and expected to come again to be left till called for, when the office opened next day? Supposing there was no mistake in the case, and Mr Murdstone had devised this plan to get rid of me, what should I do? . . . These thoughts, and a hundred other such thoughts, turned me burning hot, and made me giddy with apprehension and dismay. I was in the height of my fever when a man entered and whispered to the clerk, who presently slanted me off the scale, and pushed me over to him, as if I were weighted, bought, delivered, and paid for.

David has more grounds for panic than he knows. Already Mr. Murdstone has locked him up for five days in his room, where, already starting to internalize his confinement, he has been "ashamed" to show himself at the window, lest the boys playing in the churchyard should know that he was "a prisoner." Even when he is no longer in prison, but down in the parlor, he has retained "a sensitive consciousness of always appearing constrained." But a more awful fate awaits him at Salem House—"a square brick building with wings"—where Murdstone's discipline will be institutionalized. The placard David is there made to carry—"*Take care of him. He bites.*"—imposes on him the forfeiture of even linguistic subjectivity, its reduction to the pronoun of the non-person. (Indicatively, when David inquires about the dog, Mr. Mell replies, "that's not a dog—that's a boy," not "that's you.") David is thus linked to the closed, "close" character in the novel par excellence: "Barkis is willin' " is no worse than "he bites." It is, in fact, rather better, for Barkis has at least taken charge of his self-annulment, whereas David, obliged to wear the placard—on his back, where he can't see it—must submit to his.

> What I suffered from that placard, nobody can imagine. Whether it was possible for people to see me or not, I always fancied that somebody was reading it. It was no relief to turn around and find nobody; for wherever my back was, there I imagined somebody always to be. . . . I knew that the servants read it, and the butcher read it, and the baker read it; that everybody, in a word, who came backwards and forwards to the house, of a morning when I was ordered to walk there, read that I was to be taken care of, for I bit.

As the subject of readerly perusal unable to *look back,* David assumes the very ontology of a character in fiction. This dog's life is only trivially metamorphosed when, again under Murdstone's compulsion, he becomes "a little labouring hind in the service of Murdstone and Grinby." There his confinement is symbolized daily and in detail by the tasks he must perform. "When the empty bottles [to be rinsed, washed, examined for flaws] ran short, there were labels to be pasted on full ones, or corks to be fitted to them, or seals to be put upon the corks, or finished bottles to be packed in casks. All this work was my work." And, as though these operations were being simultaneously practiced on himself: "I mingled my tears with the water in which I was washing the bottles; and sobbed as if there were a flaw in my own breast, and it were in danger of bursting." Finally, when David forms his "great resolution" to run away to Dover, even his own box threatens to turn him into one—the kind the long-legged man calls "a pollis case." If David has "hardly breath enough to cry for the loss of [his] box," this is because, quite apart from the fact that he is exhausted from running, the box ultimately doesn't deserve his tears. All things considered, it is not a bad thing that he takes very little more out of the world, towards the retreat of his aunt, than he had brought into it.

We have already glanced at what David calls "my only and my constant comfort" throughout all this: the experience of the Novel. It begins when he happens to read the small collection of novels left by his father and impersonates his favorite characters in them, and is resumed when he recounts these novels to Steerforth at Salem House and to the other boys at Murdstone and Grinby's. It takes a still more active turn when, dejectedly lounging in obscure London streets, David fits the old books to his altered life, and makes stories for himself, out of the streets, and out of men and women. "Some points in the character I shall unconsciously develop, I suppose, in writing my life, were gradually forming all this while." From here it is an orderly progression: first to the fearful and tremulous novice who writes a little something "in secret" and sends it to a magazine; then to the writer who, Dora rightly fears, forgets her, "full of silent fancies"; and finally, to "the eminent author," as Micawber calls him, who, though "familiar to the imaginations of a considerable portion of the civilized world," nevertheless modestly occults himself in the same gesture that we saw Dickens make in the preface:

> I do not enter on the aspirations, the delights, anxieties and triumphs of my art. That I truly devoted myself to it with my strongest earnestness, I have already said. If the books I have written be of any worth, they will supply the rest. I shall otherwise have written to poor purpose, and the rest will be of interest to no one.

To the last, the experience of the novel provides David's subjectivity with a secret refuge: a free, liberalizing space in which he comes into his own, a critical space in which he takes his distance from the world's carceral oppressions. Yet if, more than anything else, this secret refuge is responsible for forming David into "the liberal subject," this is paradoxically because, in a sense, *he is not there*. Certainly, as Miss Murdstone might well have complained, David hides behind his books—but as Clara might have fondly observed, he loses himself in them as well. What has often been considered an artistic flaw in Dickens's novel—David's rather matte and colorless personality—is rather what makes the novel possible, as David's own artistic performance. Far from an aesthetic defect, the vacuity is the psychological desideratum of one whose ambition, from the time he first impersonated his favorite characters in his father's books, has always been *to be vicarious*. It is as though the only way to underwrite the self, in the sense of insuring it, were to under-write the self, in the sense of merely implying it. The Novel protects subjectivity not by locking it in, in the manner of a box, but by locking it out, since the story always determines the destiny of *somebody else*. And what goes for the subject of *David Copperfield* goes in a different dimension for the subject who reads it. He too defines his subjectivity in absentia. Entirely given over to the inner life and its meditations, constantly made to exceed the readerly determinations he both receives and practices, this subject finds himself not where he reads, but—between the lines, in the margins, outside the covers—where he does not. (Another open secret which everyone knows and no one wants to: the immense amount of daydreaming that accompanies the ordinary reading of a novel.) In this sense, the novel would be the very genre of the liberal subject, both as cause and effect: the genre that produces him, the genre to which, as its effect, he returns for "recreation."

What, then, are we to make of the fact that the experience of the Novel, alleged to take its subject out of a box, takes place in one (the "little room" at the Rookery, the "little closet" in Mr. Chillip's surgery, and so on)? The connection between the book and the box is always far closer than their effective polarity suggests. At the coaching inn, for instance, David looks at "parcels, packages, and books," and this reminds us that the book, read in a box, has the visible, palpable shape of one too. But perhaps what best "betrays" the secret consubstantiality of box and book—better than their phonetic alliteration, better than their etymological affinity (both, in a sense, coming from branches of the *same tree*)—is the article of furniture combining a chest of drawers and a writing desk that we call a bureau. At Peggotty's new home, really Barkis's old one, David is "impressed" by "a certain old bureau of dark wood in the parlour . . . with a retreating top which opened, let down, and became a desk, within which was a large quarto edition of Foxe's *Book of Martyrs*." Instead of straightforwardly ascending from box to book, the image suggests rather that one descends *en abyme* within the box through a smaller box to reach the smallest box of all, the book, where the subject at last finds himself, but only in a martyred state. What Barkis's bureau thus opens is the possibility that the book quite simply belongs to the box, as its "property" or one of its "effects."

All this is to say, in other terms, that the story of David's liberation runs parallel to the story of his submission: the chastening of what, with an ambiguous wistfulness, he calls an "undisciplined heart." The discipline from which he has escaped to become the "subject of the Novel" reappears as his own self-discipline. "What I had to do," he says of the time he labored to win Dora, "was to turn the painful discipline of my early years to account, by going to work with a steady and resolute heart." Mr. Murdstone's firmness and Mr. Creakle's unspared rod were not, it would appear, total losses. They stand behind David's victories in a succession of trials (Betsey Trotwood's "ruin," the winning of Dora, the losing of Dora) concluded and rewarded by the marriage to Agnes, the woman whom Micawber aptly calls an "appealing monitor." But what seems to ensure this self-discipline most of all is writing itself. "I could never have done what I have done, without the habits of punctuality, order, and diligence, without the determination to concentrate myself on one object at a time, no matter how quickly its successor should come upon its heels, which I then formed." Though David is not recalling here his service at Murdstone and Grinby's, but rather his apprenticeship in shorthand, he might as well be: minus the value judgments, the habits required are quite the same. It is clear as well that the discipline of writing does not lie in merely technical skills. As David's apology on the next page for the importance of being earnest confirms, these skills are immediately raised to high moral values—and these values, though differently valorized, are the very ones which help the characters to box themselves in. Paradoxically, writing is thus offered to us in *David Copperfield* as a socializing order from which the written self, always subject to omission, is separated, but with which the writing self, inevitably the agent of such omission, comes to be entirely identified.

What difference, then, is there finally between this book-loving subject and the box-like characters he would transcend? We see how ambiguous and complicated an answer to this question must be if, by way of conclusion, we consider the rather unmotivated visit that David pays to a prison at the end of the novel. With Mr. Creakle as administrator, and Uriah Heep and Mr. Littimer as model prisoners up to their old tricks, the prison scene makes some familiar points in Dickens's representation of the carceral. That the former Master of Salem House is now the magistrate in charge of a prison, as though he had merely been transferred, bears out the systemic coherence of an institutional network which fabricates the very subjects who then require its discipline. It is true that Uriah Heep's incorrigible hypocrisy would seem to be a manner of resisting the institution that seeks to restrain him, and thus of saving from discipline the subject who "puts restraints upon himself." But this secret resistance only perfects the thoroughgoing accommodation which it camouflages. Small wonder the prison has no effect in reforming Uriah, when in another, earlier version (as the "foundation school" where he and his father were raised) it has formed him in the first place. In this sense, Uriah's extravagant encomia on the prison-system—"It would be better for everybody, if they got took up, and was brought here"—belie their obvious resentment to bespeak truly the weird erotic attraction between a subject and an institution "made for each other."

The spurious opposition between Uriah and the prison is no sooner displayed, however, than it is displaced into the more authentic-seeming opposition between David and the prison. If the carceral is abruptly brought on stage at the end of the novel, when David is a respected, "untouchable" author, this is to dramatize and celebrate his distance from it: a distance that can be measured in the detached tones—and even the critical ones—

of his response. David can afford irony and indignation here because, as the pure observer, he is as free to go as he was curious to come: "We left them to their system and themselves, and went home wondering." Still, much as Uriah, the carceral subject, was fated to be matched with the prison, so David, the liberal subject, must also ensure his status with an institutional match. Not by accident is the prison scene framed, on one side, by David's realization that he loves Agnes as more than a sister, and on the other, by the actual declaration of his love to her, which prompts her to reveal her well-guarded, well-known "secret." Uriah humbly kowtows to the prison authorities; David modestly asks to be "guided" by the "appealing monitor without" (to use Micawber's distinction) who will reinforce "the silent monitor within." We can't even say that the discipline that merely befalls Uriah is David's voluntary choice, since Uriah too has chosen self-discipline, just as David has turned to account the painful discipline of his early years. Faced with the abundance of resemblances between the liberal subject and his carceral double, the home and the prison-house, how can we significantly differentiate them?

Only, I think, according to the logic of their effects, by the ways in which the two modes of discipline are played off against one another in a single system of social control. If only from the *roman noir* (but not only from it), we know that the police interrogate in teams of two. While one agent brutally attacks the suspect's body, the other more humanely appeals to his soul. The suspect is so afraid that the one will beat the guts out of him that he spills them anyway to the other. Likewise, one withdraws from the discipline of stepfathers and their institutional extensions only by turning that discipline to account, "by going to work with a steady and resolute heart." David is ultimately no different from the boxed-in characters he seeks to transcend, just as they are ultimately no different from the processes of disciplinary socialization they seek to avoid; yet in both cases, one becomes no different from the others only by, like them, assuming the effect of a difference which thus continues to operate. *David Copperfield* everywhere intimates a dreary pattern in which the subject constitutes himself against discipline by assuming that discipline in his own name. The pattern can hardly be broadcast in the novel, which requires the functioning of the difference to structure its own plot. But neither does the pattern go unbroached in the novel, whose discreet analogies remove the bar of the difference on which its very *Bildung* depends. The fact that the difference between liberal and carceral camps is not substantive, but only effective, has thus the status of a secret—that is to say, inevitably, an open secret. Accordingly, the novel must both keep this secret and give it away. Keep it, because the liberal / carceral opposition is the foundation of the liberal subject as well as the basis of the novel's own role in producing him. Give it away, because this opposition is effectively maintained by seeming always in need of maintenance—as though an impending "deconstruction" were required to inspire the anxious and incessant work of reconstructing a social order that thus keeps everyone on his toes, including the figure of the novelist who writes "far into the night." Can the game of secrecy ever be thrown in? It is not likely so long as the play remains profitable—not just to the subject whom the play allows to establish his subjectivity, but also to the social order which, playing on the play, establishes his subjection. Listen to the different voices of the police, as David does them: "That I suffered in secret, and that I suffered exquisitely, no one ever knew but I. How much I suffered, it is . . . utterly beyond my power to tell. But I kept my counsel, and I did my work.

# Containing the Destructive Work of Remembrance

*Ned Lukacher*

In November 1850, just as the last installment of *David Copperfield* appeared, Dickens wrote an article for *Household Words* about a çertain Dr. Gottfried Kinkel, who in 1848 had been a professor of theology at the University of Bonn but who now languished in a Prussian prison under a life sentence for his participation in the uprising of the spring of 1848. Dickens's purpose is to win sympathy for the much-maligned Professor Kinkel, who was clearly the victim of the hysterical atmosphere of the Prussian reaction to the events of 1848. Dickens hopes that his article will persuade men of good conscience to intervene on Kinkel's behalf and petition the Prussian government to allow Kinkel "permission to emigrate to England or America."

There is certainly nothing objectionable about Dickens's humanitarian concern in the case; as he observes, the Prussian government had plainly decided to make Kinkel an example to other middle-class intellectuals. What is objectionable is Dickens's uncritical celebration of Kinkel as the very spirit of the liberal conscience. He was not alone in falling under the professor's spell; many radicals regarded Kinkel as the incarnation of the spirit of the revolution. It was in order to dispel such delusions that Marx and Engels wrote a book entitled *The Great Men of the Exile*, the first third of which is given over to a scathing indictment of Kinkel and everything he represents. This work was written in 1852, but was not published until the twentieth century. What Marx found most objectionable about the widespread sympathy for Kinkel was that it created a romantic and highly sentimental misconception of the revolution. It is in this respect that Dickens's article is particularly culpable. He presents us with a vision of Kinkel "in sackcloth, with shaven head, and attenuated frame . . . spinning his last threads." Dickens seems to have seen in Kinkel an image of the selfless patriot he himself would like to have been:

> He sides with the Left, or democratic party; he advocates the cause of the oppressed people and the poor; he argues manfully and perseveringly the real interests of all governments, in granting a rational amount of liberty, showing that in the present stage of the moral world, it is the only thing to prevent violence, and to secure good order. His speeches breathe a prophetic spirit.

One would never guess from Dickens's account that Kinkel was a supposed revolutionary. Dickens makes him out to be something very close to a conservative Englishman, rather like himself beneath all his radical prattle. I do not know whether Dickens read Kinkel's speeches, but Marx did, and he quotes from them extensively. Far from the "prophetic spirit" Dickens appears to have heard there, Marx reveals a ridiculous poseur whose writing was filled with theological bombast and political nonsense. Dickens goes on to assure his readers that Kinkel had nothing to do with "red republicanism" and that he had joined the revolution only in order to secure for Prussia "a constitutional monarchy, like ours in England," adding enigmatically, "with such improvements as ours manifestly needs."

A few weeks after the appearance of Dickens's article, Kinkel escaped from prison and fled to England, where he visited Dickens. His escape sent a shock wave through the Prussian government. In his introduction to Marx's *Cologne Communist Trial*, Rodney Livingstone demonstrates that the escape of the celebrated Kinkel was a key factor in the government's decision to launch its conspiracy against the Communist League. The Prussians needed another scapegoat, and with Kinkel safe in England, the Communists would have to do. Livingstone cites a letter from King Frederick Wilhelm IV to his prime minister, expressing his fears for the survival of the government now that Kinkel was once again on the loose. It is indeed preposterous that the harmless professor should have sent fear and trembling into the hearts of the Prussian ruling class. It was in order to demystify the similarly hysterical atmosphere that Kinkel inspired among many of the revolutionaries themselves that Marx satirized him in *The Great Men of the Exile*.

In Marx's close stylistic analysis of his speeches, Kinkel emerges as a politico-theological pundit whose rhetorical technique is that of the blustering "*rodomontade.*" Marx writes that Kinkel's method was to inspire his students to righteousness by endowing "every little occurrence in his theologico-lyrical past" with prophetic significance. Marx points to passages where Kinkel alternately imagines that he is Noah, Elijah, even Christ. Marx on Kinkel resembles nothing so much as Swift's *Tale of a Tub,* where the rhetoric of enthusiasm is unmasked as the hideously self-indulgent farce it is. Kinkel's pietistic posturing helped to send the revolution in thc wrong direction, and it is a sign of Dickens's political naiveté that he was so easily fooled. More alarming still, Kinkel's fundamentally apolitical brand of messianic Christianity was perhaps the alternative Dickens seriously preferred to politics of any sort, radical or otherwise. Like Kinkel, Dickens was more concerned with professions of Christian sympathy for the poor than he was with concrete strategies. That Dickens should have turned to Gottfried Kinkel indicates that he was in search not of a political strategy but of a messianic revelation. In his later works Dickens depicts a world so depraved, so fallen, so far beyond the pale of political remedies that only a redeemer could save it. He constructs a muddle so dark and unreadable, a labyrinth so inescapable and defeating that it could be illuminated only by the sudden flashes of what Benjamin calls "chips of Messianic time." Dickens's admiration of Kinkel's "prophetic spirit" is finally an indication of the depth of his own political despair. In the later Dickens the personal experience of the "no thoroughfare" has become the structure of historical experience in the modern world.

Mr. Micawber anticipates the task of the *Passage Work* when he offers to assist young Copperfield in "penetrating the arcana of the modern Babylon" that was London in the 1820s. Copperfield's penetration into the dark heart of the city culminates late in the novel when, in an effort to find Emily, David and Peggotty follow her friend, the prostitute Martha Endell, into a neighborhood that was "as oppressive, sad, and solitary by night, as any about London." David calls this chapter his "night-picture," and it is indeed a Dantean vision: amidst the corruption of "strange objects, accumulated by some speculator," the riverside has been transformed into a "melancholy waste," where everything has "gradually decomposed into that nightmare condition, out of the overflowings of the polluted stream." This is where Martha has come to end her life. Like Benjamin, David is led by the prostitute into a virtually undiscovered part of the city. It is only after having reached this dark center of urban indifference that the novel's work of reparation can begin. Martha is saved, and Emily is recovered soon afterward. Here in the ebb tide where the Thames has become the River Styx, David learns that despair is the inability to forget. In the blighted stream that "creeps through the dismal streets, defiled and miserable," Martha sees an image of herself: "I know it's like me." "I have never," writes David, "known what despair was, except in the tone of those words." What Martha says of the river, "I can't forget it. It haunts me day and night," is what David feels about his ignominious past at Murdstone and Grinby's, and it is what Dickens had written of Warren's in the 1847 fragment.

The inability to forget is the great theme of *David Copperfield*. It is what compelled Dickens to restage what I am calling his primal scene [a walk through the city] in each of his novels after 1839. It is what compelled him to write the 1847 fragment, which in turn he elaborated into *David Copperfield*. We have already considered Martha Endell; besides David himself, I will also want to look closely at the character of Rosa Dartle. In each of them Dickens examines a different response to the pain of memory.

David's experience of the work of remembrance can be best presented in an early scene where he visits Micawber, who has been imprisoned for debt. Micawber is trying to be something of a politician in this scene, for he has organized the debtors to sign a petition "for an alteration in the law of imprisonment for debt." The futility of the gesture is what David finds most affecting. As he describes the prisoners filing past to sign the petition, David stops to wonder whether in the act of recollecting and writing the scene he has not sentimentalized the strange and sordid pathos it actually represents:

> I set down this remembrance here, because it is an instance to myself of the manner in which I fitted my old books to my altered life, and made stories for myself out of the streets, and out of men and women; and how some main points in the character I shall unconsciously develop, I suppose, in writing my life, were gradually forming all this while. . . . When my thoughts go back now to the slow agony of my youth, I wonder how much of the histories I invented for such people hangs like a mist of fancy over well-remembered facts! When I tread the old ground, I do not wonder that I seem to see and pity, going on before me, an innocent romantic boy, making his imaginative world out of such strange experiences and sordid things.

Dickens discovers in this extraordinary passage what Freud discovered in the 1890s when he noticed that the patient's ability to see him- or herself in the recollected scene called into question the legitimacy of the scene and offered an opportunity for the analyst to uncover other displacements and repressions. Dickens discovers further that no recollection can proceed beyond the "mist of fancy" that hangs over the ostensibly "well-remembered facts." For David, the work of remembrance is never pure; it is always derivative, already woven into the fabric of the books he has read, in this case the prison scenes in the novels of Defoe, Fielding, and Smollett. In recognizing that in the very act of writing, something is always developing "unconsciously," David recognizes and reveals the fundamental concealment, the insurmountable unreadability, at work in the act of writing and remembering.

There is another element in this passage that we have not touched on before. It is related to the growing suspicion in the later Dickens that writing itself is tainted, that a life of writing, like a political life, is a charade, a ghastly pretense without meaning or truth. David's recognition here that his memories are unreliable, and that something is always at work that makes the determination of the literal truth difficult if not impossible, is the first step in a process that will continue to intensify throughout the last twenty years of Dickens's life and will culminate in Boffin's preposterous charade as a miser in *Our Mutual Friend* and in the enigmas of *The Mystery of Edwin Drood.* David's recognition here marks an inevitably reflexive extension of the "no thoroughfare" structure to the act of composition itself. Dickens, who had long identified with the criminal, will soon see his own work as essentially criminal, for like the criminal the writer steals, misrepresents, and hoards; even worse, like an insane criminal he often perpetrates these crimes unconsciously, without even knowing what he is doing. Like those of the prisoners filing by to sign Micawber's petition, the writer's signature no longer has any legitimacy whatsoever.

Rosa Dartle is another who cannot forget the "slow agony" of her shame, the shame of having been manipulated and betrayed by Steerforth. Rosa is Dickens's most brilliant sketch of a woman scorned. The scar on her upper lip is the external mark of what David calls "some wasting fire within her." She is disfigured in a way that David finds troubling and impossible to interpret. "She brings everything to a grindstone," Steerforth says of her, "and sharpens it, as she has sharpened her own face and figure these years past. She is all edge." Her pride and her inability to accept disappointment have worn her down. She has in effect put herself to the grindstone of her own conscience. For Rosa, remembrance is destructive and disfiguring. It is through the imagery of the grindstone that we will be able to link Rosa's agonizing experience of recollection to David's.

David's stepfather is named Murdstone, and the firm he owns in London is called Mur*dstone* and *Grin*by's, which contains an anagram of Grindstone. Thinking back to the experience at Warren's Blacking is for Dickens like putting himself to the grindstone. Even Murdstone's eye, like that of several Dickensian villains, is "disfigured . . . by a cast," which is to say that he possesses the hypnotic power of the evil eye. His effect on David is to disfigure the boy's experience of memory for ever. He takes it upon himself to dull the edge of David's character. Bantering with a friend about his plan to marry David's mother, Murdstone warns his friend to be careful lest David, who is with them, should catch their drift:

> "Quinion," said Mr. Murdstone, "take care, if you please. Somebody's sharp."
>
> "Who is?" asked the gentleman, laughing.
>
> "Only Brooks of Sheffield," said Mr. Murdstone.

Sheffield is the center of the English cutlery industry. Unlike Rosa, however, David does not allow the disfiguring experiences of his past to gnaw away at his very being. The truth for Dickens was somewhere between the two. There is a great deal of Charles Dickens in Rosa Dartle. He would have preferred, no doubt, to have more David Copperfield in him than there actually was.

Chesterton, who understands so well the role of wounding in Dickens, cites a description by Mrs. Carlyle that helps me to make this link between Rosa and her creator. Mrs. Carlyle remarked that Dickens "has a face made of steel":

> This was probably felt in a flash when she saw, in some social crowd, the clear, eager face of Dickens cutting through those near him like a knife. Any people who had met him from year to year would each year have found a man weakly troubled about his worldly decline; and each year they would have found him higher up in the world. His was a character very hard for any man of slow and placable temperament to understand; he was the character whom anybody can hurt and nobody can kill.

Like Rosa, it seems that Dickens himself was "all edge."

The leitmotif of David's relationship with his stepfather is disfiguration. David's first traumatic experience occurs even before his arrival in London, when, on the occasion of being beaten by Murdstone for no reason whatsoever, David in desperation bites his torturer's hand. Murdstone is temporarily disfigured by the experience, but David is permanently so: "It was only a moment that I stopped him, for he cut me heavily an instant afterwards, and in the same instant I caught the hand with which he held me in my mouth, between my teeth, and bit it through. It set my teeth on edge to think of it." . . . It is important to note that this scene is David's primal or originary trauma. The content is certainly consistent with Dickens's interest in oral aggression, but more important than the scene itself is David's response to it. What Dickens is describing here, I believe, is the catastrophic effect of painful memories upon the mind of the child. "The fathers have eaten sour grapes, and the children's teeth are set on edge" (Ezek. 18:2). This is the line that Dickens and his readers would have heard in reading David's account. What Dickens is saying is that the disfiguring effect of painful memories is an experience no less catastrophic than hereditary sin would be. The linkage of these two ideas is itself important, and we will pursue it [elsewhere] in connection with *Little Dorrit*. In *David Copperfield*, the biting scene is the primal scene because it is this incident that disfigures David's experience of memory and his relation to his own past.

The effect of the experience on David is so disruptive that henceforth he cannot "recall how I had felt, and what sort of boy I used to be, before I bit Mr. Murdstone: which I couldn't satisfy myself about by any means, I seemed to have bitten him in such a remote antiquity." David remembers the scene; [Freud's] Rat-Man cannot. But for both of them the biting scene marks the limits of remembrance and the threshold of prehistory. It is the thought of this humiliating incident that David finds so unbearable that it sends him out of the house: "What walks I took alone, down muddy lanes, in the bad wintry weather, carrying that parlour, and Mr. and Miss Murdstone in it, everywhere: a monstrous load that I was obliged to bear, a daymare that there was no possibility of breaking in, a weight that brooded on my wits, and blunted them." "There's something in his soul," as Claudius says of Hamlet, "O'er which his melancholy sits on brood" (3.1.166–67). The pain of David's memories has "blunted" his purpose. He will never be able to escape his "daymare." But by writing, he will at least be able to sharpen his blunted wits. Like Mr. Dick—whose way of dealing with the memory of a "great disturbance and agitation," "his allegorical way of expressing it," is to write what he calls his King Charles Memorial—David also turns to writing as a way of managing or containing the destructive work of remembrance. Mr. Dick writes about a certain Charles who lost his head; Dickens must write repeatedly about the primal scene in which his experience of life was inalterably disfigured.

# Chronology

1812 Charles John Huffam Dickens, the second of eight children, is born February 7 to John and Elizabeth Dickens.

1814 John Dickens, a clerk in the Navy Pay Office, is transferred from Portsea to London. During these early years, from 1814 to 1821, Dickens is taught his letters by his mother, and he immerses himself in the fiction classics of his father's library.

1817 John Dickens moves family to Chatham.

1821 Dickens begins school with the son of a Baptist minister; he remains at this school for a time even after his family is transferred again to London in 1822.

1824 John Dickens is arrested for debt and sent to Marshalsea Prison, accompanied by his wife and younger children. Charles soon finds lodging in a poor neighborhood and begins work at Warren's Blacking Factory. His father is released three months later and Charles returns to school.

1824–26 Dickens attends Wellington House Academy, London.

1827 Works as a law clerk and spends time reading in the British Museum.

1830 Meets Maria Beadnell; he eventually falls in love with her, but she jilts him upon return from a trip to Paris in 1833.

1831 Becomes a reporter for the *Mirror of Parliament*.

1832 Becomes a staff writer for the *True Sun*.

1833 Dickens's first published piece, "A Dinner at Poplar Walk," appears in a December issue of the *Monthly Magazine* under the pen name "Boz."

1834 Dickens becomes a staff writer on the *Morning Chronicle*. His "street sketches" begin to appear in the *Evening Chronicle*. Dickens meets his future wife, Catherine Hogarth. Also, John Dickens is arrested again for debt.

| | |
|---|---|
| 1836 | *Sketches by Boz*, illustrated by George Cruikshank, published. Dickens marries Catherine Hogarth in April. Also in this year, his first play, *The Strange Gentleman,* runs for two months at the St. James's Theatre. A second play, *The Village Coquettes,* is produced at the same theater. Dickens meets John Forster, who becomes a life-long friend and his biographer. |
| 1836–37 | *Pickwick Papers* published in monthly installments from April through the following November. |
| 1837 | *Pickwick Papers* appears in book form. *Oliver Twist* begins to appear in *Bentley's Miscellany. Is She His Wife?* produced at the St. James's. Dickens's first child born, and the family moves to Doughty Street. Catherine's sister Mary, deeply loved by Dickens, dies suddenly. |
| 1838 | *Nicholas Nickleby* appears in installments; completed in October of 1839. Dickens's first daughter born. |
| 1839 | The Dickenses move to Devonshire Terrace. A second daughter born. *Nickleby* appears in book form. |
| 1840 | Dickens edits *Master Humphrey's Clock*, a weekly periodical, in which *The Old Curiosity Shop* appears. |
| 1841 | *Barnaby Rudge* appears in *Master Humphrey's Clock*. Another son born. |
| 1842 | Dickens and his wife tour America from January to June; Dickens publishes *American Notes* and begins *Martin Chuzzlewit.* |
| 1843 | *Martin Chuzzlewit* appears in monthly installments (January 1843–July 1844). *A Christmas Carol* published. |
| 1844 | Dickens tours Italy and Switzerland. Another Christmas book, *The Chimes,* completed. A third son born. |
| 1845 | Dickens produces *Every Man in his Humour* in England. *The Cricket on the Hearth* is written by Christmas, and Dickens begins *Pictures from Italy*. A fourth son born. |
| 1846 | Dickens creates and edits the *Daily News,* but resigns as editor after seventeen days. Begins *Dombey and Son* while in Lausanne; the novel appears in twenty monthly installments (October 1846–April 1848). *The Battle of Life: A Love Story* appears for Christmas. |
| 1847 | Dickens begins to manage a theatrical company and arranges a benefit tour of *Every Man in his Humour.* A fifth son born. |
| 1848 | Daughter Fanny dies. Dickens's theatrical company performs for Queen Victoria. It also performs *The Merry Wives of Wind-* |

*sor* to raise money for the preservation of Shakespeare's birthplace. Dickens's last Christmas book, *The Haunted Man,* published.

1849 Dickens begins *David Copperfield* (published May 1849–November 1850). A sixth son born.

1850 *Household Words,* a weekly periodical, established with Dickens as editor. The third daughter born, who dies within a year.

1851 Dickens and his company participate in theatrical fund-raising. Dickens's father dies.

1852 *Bleak House* appears in monthly installments (March 1852–September 1853). The first bound volume of *A Child's History of England* appears. Dickens's last child, his seventh son, born.

1853 Dickens gives first public readings, from the Christmas books. Travels to France and Italy.

1854 *Hard Times* published in *Household Words* (April 1–August 12) and appears in book form.

1855 *Little Dorrit* appears in monthly installments (December 1855–June 1857). Dickens and family travel at year's end to Paris, where the novelist meets other leading literary and theatrical persons.

1856 Dickens purchases Gad's Hill Place, and the family returns to London.

1857 Dickens is involved primarily with theatrical productions.

1858 Dickens announces his separation from his wife, about which he writes a personal statement in *Household Words.*

1859 Dickens concludes *Household Words* and establishes a new weekly, *All the Year Round. A Tale of Two Cities* appears there from April 20 to November 26, and is published in book form in December.

1860 *Great Expectations* underway in weekly installments (December 1860–August 1861).

1861 *The Uncommercial Traveller,* a collection of pieces from *All the Year Round,* published.

1862 Dickens gives many public readings and travels to Paris.

1863 Dickens continues his readings in Paris and London. Daughter Elizabeth dies.

1864 *Our Mutual Friend* appears in monthly installments for publisher Chapman and Hall (May 1864–November 1865).

1865 Dickens suffers a stroke that leaves him lame. Involved in train accident, which causes him to change the ending of *Our*

*Mutual Friend. Our Mutual Friend* appears in book form. The second collection of *The Uncommercial Traveller* published.

1866 Dickens gives thirty public readings in the English provinces.

1867 Continues the provincial readings, then travels to America in November, where he reads in Boston and New York. This tour permanently breaks the novelist's health.

1868 In April, Dickens returns to England, where he continues to tour.

1869 The first public reading of the murder of Nancy (from *Oliver Twist*) performed, but Dickens's doctors recommend he discontinue the tour. *The Mystery of Edwin Drood* begun.

1870 Dickens gives twelve readings in London. Six parts of *Edwin Drood* appear from April to September. On June 9, Charles Dickens dies, aged 58. He is buried in the Poets' Corner, Westminster Abbey.

# Contributors

HAROLD BLOOM, Sterling Professor of the Humanities at Yale University, is the author of *The Anxiety of Influence, Poetry and Repression,* and many other volumes of literary criticism. His forthcoming study, *Freud: Transference and Authority,* attempts a full-scale reading of all of Freud's major writings. A MacArthur Prize Fellow, he is general editor of five series of literary criticism published by Chelsea House. During 1987–88, he was appointed Charles Eliot Norton Professor of Poetry at Harvard University.

BARBARA HARDY is Professor of English Literature at Birkbeck College, University of London. Her books include critical studies of George Eliot and Jane Austen.

CARL BANDELIN heads the Development Office at Pitzer College of Claremont University, California.

BARRY WESTBURG is Senior Lecturer in the Department of English Language and Literature at the University of Adelaide. He is the author of *The Confessional Fictions of Charles Dickens.*

ROBERT E. LOUGY is Professor of English at Pennsylvania State University. He has received an NEH Younger Humanist Fellowship to work on twentieth-century philosophy. He has published articles on Swinburne, Morris, and Thackeray, and a book on Maturin.

JOHN P. MCGOWAN is Assistant Professor of English at the Eastman School of Music, University of Rochester.

PHILIP M. WEINSTEIN is Professor of English at Swarthmore College. His most recent book is *The Semantics of Desire: The Changing Roles of Identity from Dickens to Joyce.*

D. A. MILLER is Associate Professor of English and Comparative Literature at the University of California, Berkeley. He is the author of *Narrative and Its Discontents: Problems of Closure in the Traditional Novel*.

NED LUKACHER is Assistant Professor of English at the University of Illinois, Chicago. He is the author of *Primal Scenes: Literature, Philosophy, Psychoanalysis* and has translated two French books on Freud and psychoanalysis.

# Bibliography


Adrian, Arthur A. "*David Copperfield*: A Century of Critical and Popular Acclaim." *Modern Language Quarterly* 11 (1950): 325–31.

Black, Michael. *The Literature of Fidelity*. London: Chatto & Windus, 1975.

Bodenheimer, Rosemarie. "Dickens and the Art of Pastoral." *The Centennial Review* 23 (Fall 1979): 452–67.

Brown, Janet H. "The Narrator's Role in *David Copperfield*." *Dickens Studies Annual* 2 (1972): 197–207.

Buckley, Jerome Hamilton. *Season of Youth: The Bildungsroman from Dickens to Golding*. Cambridge: Harvard University Press, 1974.

Butt, John, and Kathleen Tillotson. *Dickens at Work*. London: Methuen, 1957.

Carey, John. *The Violent Effigy: A Study of Dickens's Imagination*. London: Faber & Faber, 1973.

Cary, Joyce. "Including Mr. Micawber." In *Selected Essays*, edited by A. G. Bishop, 172–75. London: Michael Joseph, 1976.

Chesterton, G. K. *Charles Dickens*. London: Methuen, 1906.

Churchill, R. C., comp. and ed. *Bibliography of Dickensian Criticism 1836–1975*. New York: Garland, 1975.

Cockshut, A. O. J. *The Imagination of Charles Dickens*. London: Collins, 1961.

Cohn, Alan M., and K. K. Collins. *The Cumulated Dickens Checklist 1970–1979*. Troy, New York: Whitston Publishing, 1982.

Collins, Philip. *Charles Dickens:* David Copperfield. Studies in English Literature 67. London: Edward Arnold, 1977.

———. "*David Copperfield:* 'A Very Complicated Interweaving of Truth and Fiction.' " *Essays and Studies* 23 (1970): 71–86.

———. *Dickens and Crime*. London: Macmillan, 1962.

———, ed. *Dickens: The Critical Heritage*. New York: Barnes & Noble, 1971.

Coolidge, Archibald C., Jr. *Charles Dickens as Serial Novelist*. Ames: Iowa State University Press, 1967.

Cox, C. B. "Realism and Fantasy in *David Copperfield*." *Bulletin of the John Rylands University Library* 52 (Spring 1970): 267–83.

Davis, Robert Con, ed. *The Fictional Father: Lacanian Readings of the Text*. Amherst: University of Massachusetts Press, 1981.

*Dickens Studies Annual: Essays in Victorian Fiction*. Vols. 1–7 (1970–78), Carbondale: Southern Illinois University Press. Vols. 8–13 (1980–85), New York: AMS.

*Dickens Studies Newsletter* (1970–83). Changed to *Dickens Quarterly* (1984–).

*Dickensian, The.* (1905–).

Dunn, Richard J. "*David Copperfield:* All Dickens Is There." *English Journal* 54 (1965): 789–94.

Dyson, A. E. *The Inimitable Dickens: A Reading of the Novels.* London: Macmillan, 1970.

Fenstermaker, John J. *Charles Dickens, 1940–1975: An Analytical Subject Index to Periodical Criticism of the Novels and Christmas Books.* Boston: G. K. Hall, 1979.

Fleishman, Avrom. "The Fictions of Autobiographical Fiction." *Genre* 9 (Spring 1976): 73–86.

Ford, George H. *Dickens and His Readers: Aspects of Novel Criticism since 1836.* Princeton: Princeton University Press, 1955.

Ford, George H., and Lauriat Lane, Jr., eds. *The Dickens Critics.* Ithaca, N.Y.: Cornell University Press, 1961.

Forster, John. *The Life of Charles Dickens.* Edited by A. J. Hoppe. 2 vols. London: J. M. Dent, 1966.

Garis, Robert E. *The Dickens Theatre: A Reassessment of the Novels.* Oxford: Clarendon Press, 1965.

Gold, Joseph. *Charles Dickens: Radical Moralist.* Minneapolis: University of Minnesota Press, 1972.

Graves, Robert. *The Real* David Copperfield. London: Baker, 1933.

Grundy, Dominick E. "Growing Up Dickensian." *Literature and Psychology* 22, no. 2 (1972): 99–106.

Hall, William F. "Caricature in Dickens and James." *University of Toronto Quarterly* 39 (April 1970): 242–57.

Hardy, Barbara. *The Moral Art of Dickens.* New York: Oxford University Press, 1970.

Hirsch, Gordon D. "A Psychoanalytic Rereading of *David Copperfield.*" *Victorian Newsletter* 58 (Fall 1980): 1–5.

House, Humphry. *The Dickens World.* London: Oxford University Press, 1941.

Hughes, Felicity. "Narrative Complexity in *David Copperfield.*" *ELH* 41 (1974): 89–105.

Hurley, Edward. "Dickens's Portrait of the Artist." *Victorian Newsletter* 38 (Fall 1970): 1–5.

Johnson, Edgar. *Charles Dickens: His Tragedy and Triumph.* New York: Simon & Schuster, 1952.

Kincaid, James. *Dickens and the Rhetoric of Laughter.* Oxford: Clarendon Press, 1971.

Lankford, William T. " 'The Deep of Time': Narrative Order in *David Copperfield.*" *ELH* 46 (1979): 452–67.

Leavis, F. R., and Q. D. Leavis. *Dickens the Novelist.* London: Chatto & Windus, 1970.

Lerner, Laurence. *Love and Marriage: Literature and Its Social Context.* London: Edward Arnold, 1979.

Manheim, Leonard. "The Personal History of David Copperfield." *American Imago* 9 (1953): 23–43.

Marcus, Steven. *The Other Victorians: A Study of Sexuality and Pornography in Mid-Nineteenth-Century England.* New York: New American Library, 1977.

Marshall, William H. "The Image of Steerforth and the Structure of *David Copperfield*." *Tennessee Studies in Literature* 5 (1960): 57–66.

Miller, J. Hillis. *Charles Dickens: The World of His Novels*. Cambridge: Harvard University Press, 1958.

Monod, Sylvère. *Dickens the Novelist*. Norman: University of Oklahoma Press, 1968.

Needham, Gwendolyn B. "The Undisciplined Heart of David Copperfield." *Nineteenth-Century Fiction* 9 (Sept. 1954): 81–107.

Orwell, George. "Charles Dickens." In *Dickens, Dali and Others: Studies in Popular Culture*, 1–75. New York: Reynal and Hitchcock, 1946.

Patten, Robert L. "Autobiography into Autobiography: The Evolution of *David Copperfield*." In *Approaches to Victorian Autobiography*, edited by George P. Landow, 269–90. Athens: Ohio University Press, 1979.

Pearlman, E. "David Copperfield Dreams of Drowning." *American Imago* 28 (1971): 391–403.

Spengemann, William C. *The Forms of Autobiography: Episodes in the History of a Literary Genre*. New Haven: Yale University Press, 1980.

Spilka, Mark. "*David Copperfield* as Psychological Fiction." *Critical Quarterly* 1 (Winter 1959): 292–301.

Stoehr, Taylor. *Dickens: The Dreamer's Stance*. Ithaca, N.Y.: Cornell University Press, 1965.

Stone, Harry. *Dickens and the Invisible World: Fairy Tales, Fantasy, and Novel-Making*. Bloomington: Indiana University Press, 1979.

Sucksmith, Harvey Peter. *The Narrative Art of Charles Dickens: The Rhetoric of Sympathy and Irony in His Novels*. Oxford: Clarendon Press, 1970.

Talbot, Norman. "The Naming and the Namers of the Hero: A Study in *David Copperfield*." *Southern Review* 11 (1978): 267–82.

Tick, Stanley. "The Memorializing of Mr. Dick." *Nineteenth-Century Fiction* 24 (1969): 142–53.

Vogel, Jane. *Allegory in Dickens*. Studies in the Humanities 17. University: University of Alabama Press, 1977.

Welsh, Alexander. *The City of Dickens*. Oxford: Clarendon Press, 1971.

Westburg, Barry. *The Confessional Fictions of Charles Dickens*. De Kalb: Northern Illinois University Press, 1977.

Williams, Raymond. *The English Novel from Dickens to Lawrence*. London: Chatto & Windus, 1970.

Wilson, Angus. *The World of Charles Dickens*. New York: Viking, 1970.

Wilson, Edmund. "The Two Scrooges." In *The Wound and the Bow*, 3–85. Cambridge: Houghton, 1941.

Woolf, Virginia. "*David Copperfield*." In *The Moment and Other Essays*, 75–80. London: Hogarth, 1947.

Worth, George. *Dickensian Melodrama*. University of Kansas Humanistic Studies 50. Lawrence: University of Kansas, 1978.

# Acknowledgments

"The Moral Art of Dickens: *David Copperfield*" (originally entitled "*David Copperfield*") by Barbara Hardy from *The Moral Art of Dickens* by Barbara Hardy, © 1970 by Barbara Hardy. Reprinted by permission of the author and Oxford University Press.

"*David Copperfield:* A Third Interesting Penitent" by Carl Bandelin from *Studies in English Literature 1500–1900* 16, no. 4 (Autumn 1976), © 1976 by William Marsh Rice University. Reprinted by permission.

"David Sees 'Himself' in the Mirror" (originally entitled "*David Copperfield* and the Aesthetics of Education") by Barry Westburg from *The Confessional Fictions of Charles Dickens* by Barry Westburg, © 1977 by Northern Illinois University Press, De Kalb, Illinois. Reprinted by permission.

"Remembrances of Death Past and Future: A Reading of *David Copperfield*" by Robert E. Lougy from *Dickens Studies Annual* 6 (1976), © 1979 by AMS Press, Inc. Reprinted by permission.

"*David Copperfield:* The Trial of Realism" by John P. McGowan from *Nineteenth-Century Fiction* 34, no. 1 (June 1979), © 1979 by the Regents of the University of California. Reprinted by permission.

"Mr. Peggotty and Little Em'ly: Misassessed Altruism?" by Philip M. Weinstein from *The Semantics of Desire: Changing Models of Identity from Dickens to Joyce* by Philip M. Weinstein, © 1984 by Princeton University Press. Reprinted by permission of Princeton University Press.

"Secret Subjects, Open Secrets" by D. A. Miller from *Dickens Studies Annual* 14 (1985), © 1985 by AMS Press, Inc. Reprinted by permission.

"Containing the Destructive Work of Remembrance" (originally entitled "Dialectical Images: Benjamin/Dickens/Freud") by Ned Lukacher from *Primal Scenes: Literature, Philosophy, Psychoanalysis* by Ned Lukacher, © 1986 by Cornell University. Reprinted by permission of Cornell University Press.

# Index


*Adam Bede* (George Eliot), 68
Adorno, T. W., 100
Aesthetics: of *David Copperfield* and *Great Expectations,* 36, 46; Dickens's, 4, 7; and narcissicism, 40, 41; of pleasure, 4, 5–6
Agnes, *See* Wickfield, Agnes
Artist, the, 37; as child, 47, 48, 52; fictions of, 46; Romantic, 48, 63; Victorian concept of, 10–11
Autobiography: and the novel, 95; *The Personal History of David Copperfield* as, 5, 6, 8, 9, 15, 16, 40, 89, 92, 93, 95, 103. *See also David Copperfield, The Personal History of.*

Barkis, Mr: and box imagery, 95, 104, 106; self-effacement of, 96
Beadnell, Maria, and Dora Spenlow, 16
Bennett, Arnold, 16
Bildungsroman, *David Copperfield* as, 9, 14, 21, 108–9
Blake, William, 85
Body, the: David's discovery of, 33, 34–35, 42
Borges, Jorge Luis, 44
Box, as image, 95–97, 100, 103, 105–7, 108
Brontë, Charlotte, 15–16, 34–35
Brown, Janet, 86

Characters: in *David Copperfield,* 18, 76, 95–97, 98–99, 100–1, 103; in Dickens's fiction, 2, 4, 13, 18, 22. *See also entries for specific characters*
Charles I, King, 47, 49–50. *See also* Dick, Mr; Memorial
Chesterton, G. K., 13, 116
Child: artist as, 48, 52; David and Dora's, 77; *David Copperfield* as Dickens's, 6, 9, 46; Mr Dick as, 48. *See also* Childhood; Children
Childhood, 16, 40; David's 7, 13, 15, 22, 32–35, 53, 54, 70, 73–74, 75, 78, 92–94, 116, 117; Dickens's treatment of, 13, 15, 38–39; identity crises in, 32; images from, 52, 53, 54, 56, 57. *See also* Child; Children
Children: Dickens on, 48; fantasy and, 85; fascination with words of, 75; Lacan on, 34, 36–37; Merleau-Ponty on, 37, 38–39; perception of time of, 77, 78. *See also* Childhood; Child
Child-wife, Dora Spenlow as, 12, 27, 83; Clara Murdstone as, 83
Chillip, Mr, 96
Comedy, in *David Copperfield,* 6, 16, 17, 18–19, 30, 79
Consciousness: acquired, 24; childhood crises of, 31; David's development of, 21–22; growth of, 31; imaginary, 37; the reader's, 100
Copperfield, David: and Agnes Wickfield, 7, 17, 21, 28, 29, 30, 46, 63, 98, 108; attitudes toward language of, 73, 74–77, 78, 80; and Clara Murdstone, 39, 40, 69, 92–93; crises of, 31, 32, 33, 38, 39, 43–45, 52–57; Dark Night of the Soul of, 22–23, 26, 28, 29; and Dora Spenlow, 10, 24, 26–27, 43, 77, 78, 83; dreams of, 71; and Edward Murdstone, 7, 32–33, 35,

Copperfield, David *(continued)* 38, 39, 73–74, 114, 116–17; egocentricity of, 22, 28, 29–30; fantasies of, 24, 25, 26, 27; grief of, 22, 23, 28, 94, 103, 104, 107, 109; guilt feelings of, 22–24, 25, 26, 28, 30, 33, 35, 39, 103; infatuation with Emily of, 24–25, 45; and James Steerforth, 24–26, 43, 44–45; journey to Switzerland of, 22, 28, 61, 62; liberation and submission of, 106; and Nature, 16, 62–63; as novelist, 6, 8, 10–11, 36, 40, 47–48, 57, 65, 78, 94–95, 102, 104–6, 107, 117; penitence of, 21, 28, 29, 30; psychological development of, 21, 22–23, 28–30, 31, 62; undisciplined heart of, 13, 14, 15, 17–18, 28, 31, 36, 68–69, 106. *See also* Childhood

Creakle, Mr, 29, 30

Dartle, Rosa: anger against Emily of, 49, 85–86; Charles Dickens compared to, 116; and James Steerforth, 115; memory and, 114, 115

*David Copperfield, The Personal History of*, 13, 14, 31; alienation in, 51, 65; as autobiography, 5, 6, 8, 9, 15, 16, 40, 89, 92, 93, 95, 103; as bildungsroman, 9, 14, 21, 108–9; comedy in, 6, 16, 17, 18–19, 21; conclusion of, 52, 64–65; educational aspects of, 36, 40; fantasy in, 15–16, 71; Freudian aspects of, 5, 6, 8, 17, 85, 98, 99, 100, 114, 117; imagery in, 16, 34, 36–38, 44–46, 47, 50, 52, 54, 56, 57, 60, 62, 64–65, 66, 71, 72, 95–98, 100, 107, 115–16; imagination in, 31–32, 35, 39, 46; introspection vs. action in, 52, 59–61; limitations of, 7, 14, 16, 21; memory in, 31–32, 53, 66, 114–15; nature of characters in, 18, 76, 95–97, 98–99, 100–1, 103; perceptual experience in, 69–71, 75, 77; readers' reaction to, 12, 13, 99, 100–1; realism in, 15–16, 68, 73; secrecy in, 94–95, 97, 98–100, 108; specific chapters in: "Absence," 61–63; "Domestic," 14–15; "I Observe," 69; "Tempest," 52–57, 62; themes in, 7, 19, 33, 35, 41–42, 48, 50, 52, 53–54, 59, 60–61, 62, 94, 103, 104, 107, 114; unity of, 13, 19; Victorian aspects of, 9–10, 11, 12, 15, 49, 51, 59, 60, 100–1. *See also entries for specific characters.*

Death, 13, 55, 56, 57, 60, 65, 70, 73, 76, 77, 115; of Clara Murdstone, 41, 79, 83; of David and Dora's child, 77; David's fear of, 52–53, 54, 56; of Dora Spenlow, 12, 15, 22, 24, 27, 41, 81, 88; of Ham, 22, 23, 26, 27, 28, 41, 52, 56–57, 88; of James Steerforth, 22, 41, 52, 56–57

Demonic the, 50, 52, 59–60, 66

Derrida, Jacques, 68

Dick, Mr: alienation of, 51; childlikeness of, 48; handwriting of, 76; and King Charles Memorial, 47, 48, 49, 50–51, 117; madness of, 47, 48, 49, 51

Dickens, Charles: childhood of, 94, 114, 116; marriage of, 15, 16; political views of, 112–14; relationship to *David Copperfield* of, 6, 8, 9, 40, 46, 91–92; Rosa Dartle compared to, 116. *See Also* Autobiography

Dickens, Catherine, 16

Dickens's fiction, 13; caricature in, 2, 18; childhood in, 13, 31, 38–39; father/lover figures in, 84, 85; Freudian aspects of, 5, 6, 8, 17, 85; growth of consciousness in, 31; Henry James on, 1–2; human will in, 5, 8; John Ruskin on, 2–3; nature of characters in, 2, 4, 13, 18, 22; originality of, 5, 6; readers' reaction to, 12–13; self-preoccupation in, 22; Shakespearean quality of, 3–4; Victorian aspects of, 9–12; Works: *Bleak House*, 8, 13, 18, 22, 64; *Great Expectations*, 10, 23–24, 38, 58, 62, 64; *Hard Times*, 2, 22, 33, 64, 67, 68; *Haunted Man, The*, 40; *Little Dorrit*, 1, 22, 64; *Mystery of Edwin Drood, The*, 84, 115; *Our Mutual Friend*, 1, 22, 62, 115. *See also David Copperfield, The Personal History of; Sketches by Boz*

Disfiguration: of David, 116–17; of Rosa Dartle, 115
*Double, The* (Dostoyevski), 46
Dreams, in *David Copperfield,* 71–72

*Ecrits: A Selection* (Lacan), 34–35
Eliot, George, 13, 15, 31, 68
Eliot, T. S., on Dickens's characters, 4
Emigration: of the Micawbers, 7, 22; of Peggotty and Emily, 7, 22, 27, 28, 87–88, 95
Em'ly, Little, 7, 10; Christian forgiveness and, 86–87; David's infatuation with, 24–25, 45; engagement to Ham of, 83–84; as fallen woman, 88, 113; and Peggotty, 83–88, 113; Rosa Dartle's anger against, 85–86, 87; Steerforth's seduction of, 10, 24, 25, 26, 49, 84–85, 88, 113
Endell, Martha, 113–14
Eroticism, and narcissicism, 43, 44

Fancy: aesthetic of, 67; in David's writing, 69; and fact, 68; and realism, 67, 68, 82
Fantasy: in *David Copperfield,* 15–16, 71; and event, 24, 25–26; of lost children, 85; and realism, 15
Father: Dickens as David's, 6; as husband/lover, 84, 85; Peggotty as, 88
Faulkner, William, 85
Feeling: and the comic, 18; demands on, 12–13; and fantasy, 16; unity of, 19
Fiction: artists' lives as, 46; and the real, 67
Freud, and *David Copperfield,* 5, 6, 8, 17, 85, 98, 100, 114, 117

Garden, as image, 60, 64–65
Guilt, David's feelings of, 22–24, 25, 26, 28, 30, 33, 35, 39, 103
Grief, David's, 22, 23, 28, 94, 103, 104, 107, 109
*Great Men of Exile, The* (Karl Marx and Friedrich Engels), 111, 112
Gummidge, Mrs, and Peggotty, 87

Hardy, Barbara, 21
Hartman, Geoffrey, 62
Heep, Uriah, 7, 96–97; character of, 11, 61, 96–97, 99; and David Copperfield, 17; downfall and denunciation of, 11, 61, 81–82; in prison, 29, 107–8
History: and the present, 19; repetition of in writing, 78
Hoffman, E. T. A., 46
Houses, as image, 34, 44, 54
*Household Words,* 67, 111
Hume, David, on images, 71

Identity: David's crisis of, 32, 33, 45; Dickens's, 44, 46
Images and imagery: artists' creation of, 47–48, 52; box, 95–98, 103, 106; of childhood, 53, 54, 57; Desert of Sahara, 64–65; dream, 51–52, 71–72; of enclosure, 60, 65 garden, 60, 64–65; house, 34, 44, 54; grave, 47–48; grindstone, 115–16; King Charles, 49–50; in later novels, 64; mirrors, 34–35, 36–37, 38, 39, 40, 42–43, 44, 45; ship, 49–50; in "Tempest" chapter, 52, 56, 57. *See also* Metaphor
Imagination: artistic, 35; linguistic, 19; as theme in *David Copperfield,* 31–32, 35, 39, 46

James, Henry, 4, 5, 14; on Dickens, 1–2
*Jane Eyre* (C. Brontë): mirrors as image in, 34–35; realism and fantasy in, 15–16
Johnson, Edgar, 6, 13
Jonson, Ben, 1, 3
Journey: David's through memory, 48, 50, 53; David's to Switzerland, 22, 28, 61, 62; Peggotty's, 60–61; "Tempest" chapter and, 52, 53–54; time and, 59; *See also* Pilgrimage
Joyce, James, 5, 12

Kinkel, Dr Gottfried: Dickens's defense of, 111–12; Marx's analysis of, 112–13
Knowledge: and the novel, 57; secrecy and, 99–100

Lacan, Jacques: on infants, 34, 36; on "chain of desire," 79
Lane, Margaret, 16
Langbaum, Robert, 38
Language: David's attitude toward, 73, 74–77, 78, 80; and meaning, 77–78; of Micawber and Murdstone, 73–74, 75; as reinterpretation of world, 80; and time, 76–77
Leavis, Q. D., 29, 85
Littimer, 29, 96
Loss: David's, 22, 23, 26, 27, 77; language and, 76, 77, 78; time and, 79–80
Madness: Mr Dick's, 47, 48, 49, 51; Mrs Steerforth's, 47, 48; Victorian attitude toward, 49, 50; and writing, 51–52
Marriage, 14, 15; of Agnes and David, 46, 63; Dickens's, 15, 16; of Dora and David, 26–27, 77; of the Murdstones, 83; of the Strongs, 80
*Mill on the Floss* (G. Eliot), 15–16
Mills, Julia, 64
Memorial: David's, 47, 48, 57; Mr Dick's, 48, 49, 50, 51, 117
Memory: David's, 66, 68, 80; and dreams, 71–72; past and present in, 72; and repetition, 78–79; as theme in *David Copperfield*, 18–19, 31–32, 39, 113–17; as way of seeing, 69, 71, 72
Merleau-Ponty, Maurice, on infants and children, 36–37, 38–39
Metaphor: of David as dog, 103, 104; of garden of Eros, 60; horseback rides as, 30; madness as, 49, Nature as, 62–63; ship as, 49–50; storm at Yarmouth as, 54–55. *See also* Images and Imagery
Micawber, Mr, 7, 18; as John Dickens, 6, 16; language of, 73–74, 75, 81; in prison, 114; and Uriah Heep, 61, 81–82
Micawber, Mrs, 18
Mirror, as image, 34–35, 36–37, 38, 39, 40, 42–43, 44, 45, 46; and children, 34–35, 36–37
Monod, Sylvère, 21
Mowcher, Miss, 25
Murdstone, Clara, 39, 40, 69, 83, 92–93
Murdstone, Edward: and David, 7, 32–33, 35, 38, 39, 73–74, 114, 116–17; and Grinby, 116; language of, 73–74

Narcissism: and aesthetics, 40, 41; and the artist, 37–38; and mirror images, 44; and personal relationships, 32; of symbols, 35
Narrative, 6, 14, 71
Narrator: in *David Copperfield*, 102–13; in *Sketches by Boz*, 101–2
Needham, Gwendolyn, 13
Newsom, Robert, 67
Novel, the: autobiographical, 9, 15, 40; of education, 9, 14; as genre, 106; of memory, 118, 119; psychological, 15, 16–17; rhythm of, 19; tradition of, 66, 67

Past, the; 18, 19; artist and, 48; King Charles's image and, 47, 48; in the present, 73, 80, 82
Peggotty, Ham: betrayal of by Steerforth, 84, 85; death of, 22, 23, 26, 27, 28; Emily's engagement to, 83
Peggotty, Mr, 7, 49, 76; emigration of, 27, 28, 87–88, 95; as father/lover figure, 83–85, 87–88; journey of as pilgrimage, 60–61; rescue of Emily of, 85–87, 113
Penitence, David's, 21, 28, 29, 30
Pilgrimage: David's, 57, 61–62; and language and metaphor, 62–63; Mr Peggotty's, 60–61
*Portrait of a Lady, The* (James), 14
Present, the: historic, 19; and the past, 73, 80, 82; and the child, 77
Price, Martin, 77
Prison: Creakle's model, 29, 30; David's at Salem House, 103; David's visit to, 107, 108; Micawber in, 114; reform of, 10, 21; in *Sketches by Boz*, 40–41

Rank, Otto, 37
Realism: critique of, 75; and fancy, 15–16, 68, 73; time and, 73, 76
Repetition: literary realism and, 76; memory and, 78–79; Mr Micawber and, 81–82
Ruskin, John, 2–3

Sartre, Jean-Paul, 37–38
Secrecy, 90–91, 99; in *David Copperfield*, 94–95, 97, 98–100, 108; open secrets and, 98, 100, 106, 109; writing and, 94–95
Self, 66; alienation from, 65; David's denial of, 21–22, 27, 28, 30; David's preoccupation with, 22, 28, 29, 30, 39, 40, 44, 63; development of, 35; Dickens's representation of, 8; discipline of, 96, 106–7; knowledge of, in Dickens's fiction, 14; and writing, 94–95, 107
Separation: of individual from society, 49; terror of, 57
Ship: as metaphor, 49–50; as Peggotty's home, 54
*Sketches by Boz*: character and narrator in, 101; imprisonment in, 40–41; lack of adventure in, 101; subject and object in, 102
Spenlow, Dora, 7, 16, 96; and Agnes, 15, 17; as child-wife, 12, 27, 83; and David, 10, 14–15, 17, 24, 26, 27, 43, 77; death of, 24, 26, 27, 81
"Stage fire," Dickens's, 3, 5, 7, 8
Steerforth, James, 7, 58; and David, 17, 44–45, 93–94; death of, 22, 23, 26, 27; mother of, 47, 48; and Rosa Dartle, 115; seduction of Emily of, 24, 25, 84, 85
Storm, at Yarmouth, 26, 43–44, 53–54
Strong, Annie, 13, 14
Subjectivity, 90, 91, 101, 109; characters' protection of, 96–97, 98; David's, 105; Dickens's, 92; displaced, 95; and objectivity, 44; preface and, 92
Suffering, 7; David's, 41–42, 94, 103, 104, 105; and grief, David's, 22, 23, 28, 94, 103, 104, 107, 109; physical, 35
Swift, Jonathan, 3

*Tale of a Tub, A* (Swift), 113
Time, 19, 58, 59; children and, 77, 78; and realism, 73, 76; language and, 77; memory in, 80; and loss, 79–80
Traddles, Thomas, 30, 76, 96; and Mr Dick's writings, 50–51; history of, 60; and Uriah Heep, 61
Trotwood, Aunt Betsey, 7, 18; and box imagery, 95, 96, 97; and Mr Dick, 49, 51; past history of, 81
Vision: of the novel, 63; daytime vs. nighttime, 69–70, 71; Mr Dick and, 52; final, 63–64; hero's private, 57–58; public and private, 59

Whitman, Walt, 1
Wickfield, Agnes, 7, 12; as agent of David's recovery, 21, 27, 28–29; and David, 7, 17, 21, 27, 28–29, 30, 46, 63, 98, 108; and Dora, 15, 17
Words, 68; appearance of, 75–76; David's attitude towards, 73, 75–76; denunciation of, 74; and handwriting, 76; Micawber and, 74, 75, 81; significance of, 78, 81
Wordsworth, William, 48, 62
World: characters' battle with, 96; of child, 77, 78; consciousness of outer, 70; of *David Copperfield*, 57 60; Dickens's, 113; man's place in 62; of Micawber and Murdstone, 73–74; in words, 68
Writing: Dickens's attitude toward, 65–66; importance to David of, 6, 8, 10–11, 36, 40, 47–48, 65, 78, 94–95, 102, 104–5, 106–7, 117; and Mr Dick, 51, 115, 117

Yarmouth: and Peggotty household, 39; storm at, 26, 52, 54–55, 56

## VIVA Modern Critical Interpretations

### Available Titles in the Series

**Alice's Adventures in Wonderland**

9788130906362 Rs. 145

**Animal Farm**

9788130906355 In Print

**As You Like It**

9788130918723 Rs. 195

**The Adventures of Huckleberry Finn**

9788130907390 Rs. 165

**Beowulf**

9788130907406 In Print

**Beloved**

9788130918884 Rs. 195

**Black Boy**

9788130906737 Rs. 125

**Brave New World**

9788130906348 In Print

**Cat on a Hot Tin Roof**

9788130906393 Rs. 99

# VIVA Modern Critical Interpretations®

## Available Titles in the Series

Viva

**Crime and Punishment**

9788130906409 Rs. 175

**The Chronicles of Narnia**

9788130907468 Rs. 145

**The Crucible**

9788130906416 Rs. 125

**Darkness at Noon**

9788130906423 Rs. 145

**David Copperfield**

9788130918730 Rs. 145

**The Death of Artemio Cruz**

9788130907475 Rs. 145

**Death of a Salesman**

9788130906744 Rs. 125

**The Divine Comedy**

9788130918846 Rs. 175

**Don Quixote**

9788130904658 Rs. 125

# VIVA Modern Critical Interpretations

## Available Titles in the Series

Viva

**The Great Gatsby**

9788130906454 Rs. 145

**Gulliver's Travels**

9788130906461 Rs. 195

**Hamlet**

9788130918877 Rs. 165

**The Iliad**

9788130907895 Rs. 145

**Invisible Man**

9788130906485 In Print

**Heart of Darkness**

9788130918815 Rs. 165

**Jane Eyre**

9788130918860 Rs. 195

**Julius Caesar**

9788130906492 Rs. 125

**King Lear**

9788130918853 Rs. 165

# VIVA Modern Critical Interpretations

## Available Titles in the Series

Viva

**Long Day's Journey into Night**

9788130904634 Rs. 99

**Lord of the Flies**

9788130904603 Rs. 145

**The Lord of the Rings**

9788130907956 Rs. 145

**The Man without Qualities**

9788130907499 Rs. 145

**The Merchand of Venice**

9788130906522 In Print

**Macbeth**

9788130906515 Rs. 125

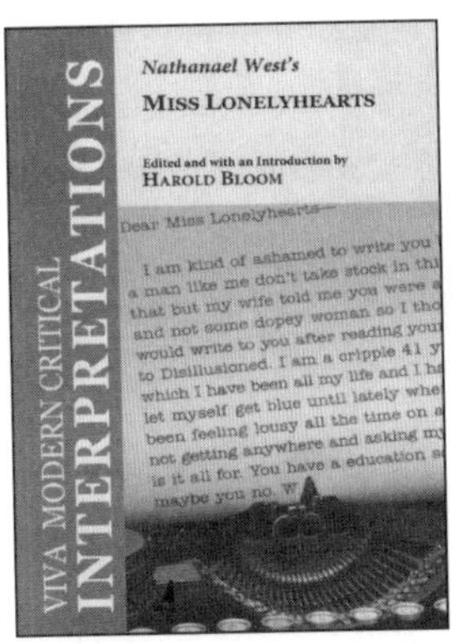


**Miss Lonelyhearts**

9788130907437 Rs. 125

**A Midsummer Night's Dream**

9788130918914 Rs. 165

**The Metamorphosis**

9788130904573 Rs. 99

## VIVA Modern Critical Interpretations

### Available Titles in the Series

Viva

**Moby-Dick**

9788130906546 Rs. 165

**Oedipus**

9788130906768 Rs. 165

**One Flew Over the Cuckoo's Nest**

9788130907444 Rs. 125

**One Hundred Years of Solitude**

9788130907451 In Print

**The Old Man and the Sea**

9788130906553 Rs. 125

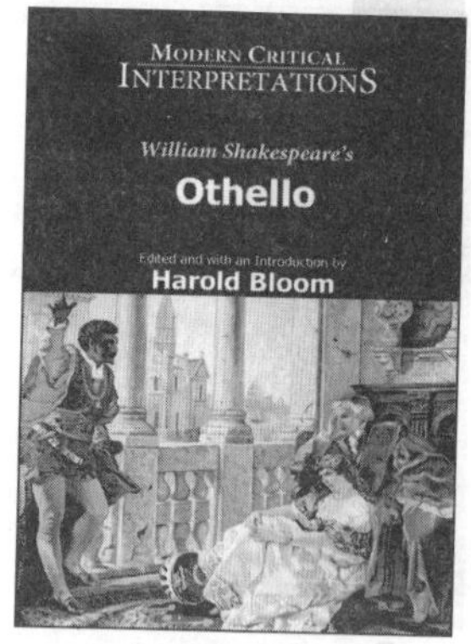


**Othello**

9788130918891 Rs. 165

**Paradise Lost**

9788130906560 In Print

**The Pardoner's Tale**

9788130904665 Rs. 125

**A Passage to India**

9788130906584 Rs. 145

# VIVA Modern Critical Interpretations

## Available Titles in the Series

Viva

**Persuasion**

9788130906591 Rs. 175

**Pride and Prejudice**

9788130906607 Rs. 195

**The Red Badge of Courage**

9788130906614 Rs. 145

**Romeo and Juliet**

9788130906621 In Print

**The Rubaiyat of Omar Khayyam**

9788130904641 Rs. 145

**The Scarlet Letter**

9788130907505 Rs. 175

**Silas Marner**

9788130906638 Rs. 125

**Song of Solomon**

9788130906645 Rs. 145

**Sophie's Choice**

9788130906652 Rs. 175

# VIVA Modern Critical Interpretations

## Available Titles in the Series

**The Sound and The Fury**

9788130906676 Rs. 195

**A Streetcar Named Desire**

9788130918716 Rs. 145

**Sonnets**

9788130918907 Rs. 165

**A Tale of Two Cities**

9788130906683 Rs. 145

**The Tempest**

9788130918822 Rs. 175

**To Kill a Mockingbird**

9788130906775 Rs. 125

**Waiting for Godot**

9788130906706 Rs. 99

**Ulysses**

9788130906690 Rs. 145

**The Waste Land**

9788130904689 Rs. 175

**Wuthering Heights**

9788130906713 Rs. 175

**Young Goodman Brown**

9788130906720 Rs. 125